The Method of Surrendering
A Reader's Guide

Michael Barron Ph.D.

ISBN: 10: 0-9989990-6-7
ISBN-13: 978-0-9989990-6-7
Extravagant Promises Press

INTRODUCTION

We are all born of the spirit. Our soul is but a guidebook inspired by God's divine plan. Our souls are only an element in the great plan. Here is an invitation to breathe the vivid, to feel the fire in the hearts center and join the journey into full flowing spirit of heaven on earth.

THE METHOD OF SURRENDERING

TABLE OF CONTENTS

LIST OF ILLUSTRATIONS

ABOUT THE AUTHOR

Michael C. Barron has been a professor of education at the University level with Masters' degrees in education, art and design. Additional works include an advanced doctoral degree in health, medical sports training and coaching. His expertise has been in the field of coaching football, sports training and therapy. For over 35 years he has taught at the university and secondary levels. He has a lifelong career of helping, teaching and coaching students at all levels of education.

Michael C. Barron is dedicated to service within a twelve-step program, and in the observation of drug and alcohol addiction. This is Barron's second publication. He is the exclusive author of "The Method of Forgiveness," published in 2010.

vi

FIRST FOREWORD

The Method of Surrendering

One is not an innocent victim of one's environment. Each person on earth is responsible for the circumstance in which they find themselves. It is simply an act of "meeting self."

"What ye sow, ye reap."

The act of "meeting self," according to this book "Method of Surrendering," shows us how to meet and greet the consequences of our attitude and actions. This "meeting self," or the revelation of consequences includes previous thoughts and emotions we have brought about. We make choices. Choices based in former judgment situations. Choices for which we are responsible. Meaning we make choices based on previous experiences; good, bad, or indifferent. We are free to choose the consequences of our choices and actions. And we must face every jot and tittle. We cannot escape.

It is the purpose of this book to find a fundamental approach to learning how to forgive ourselves and others, to look at reality for reality's sake (accepting the good, bad, and indifferent), and to make each day a better day with God and His plan.

SECOND FOREWORD

From Surrendering to Surrendered

I had just recently been released from the hospital, having completed a carotid artery surgery. After having spent five days in the hospital I was looking forward to going home for a good night's sleep.

The eighth day after surgery, I woke up around 7:00 AM and prepared myself to go downstairs. I proceeded to walk down the flight of stairs and at the bottom I remembered that I needed my cell phone. I turned and went back up the flight of stairs, grabbed my phone and proceeded back downstairs. I was at the bottom of the stairs, standing on the very last step. I felt a slight tear and an immediate pain in my neck. In an instant, I knew I was bleeding internally.

I can only describe what I recall as a quick tear and a woosh sound. The pain in my neck and hearing this noise in my head, I knew I was in trouble. I immediately called 911 and requested that an ambulance be sent to my house at once.

After making the 911 call, I went to the front door and opened it. All the while I was grabbing, grasping and holding onto my neck as blood started to gush on the inside. I knew this because I felt it. I laid down on the living room floor and waited for the ambulance to arrive.

After about seven minutes the police department and the fire department arrived at my house and entered my front door. After finding me down on the carpet they asked me what was wrong. I tried to explain, as best I could, that I had just completed carotid artery surgery and that the vein or valve had burst and that I was bleeding internally.

At the time, there was nothing the fire department could do for me. Luckily the paramedics arrived, put me on a gurney and into the ambulance. Then we were off to the hospital.

There I was in an ambulance being driven to San Antonio hospital in Upland, California. The ride from my home in Chino Hills to Upland was approximately 20 minutes. If I were to guess, I'd say the driver was doing 70 mph.

There was one moment that I recall asking the paramedics to put pressure on my neck and to help me with my breathing. In that moment I didn't know which was worse; the excruciating pain and pressure from the paramedic's hands, or not being able to breathe.

We arrived at the hospital, literally hitting the emergency room doors as I struggled to breathe. I knew in my heart that I'd be dead in five minutes. With the revelation that death was imminent I simply asked my God (my higher power) to wait for me. I would see him in the next minute with no remorse, no fear, no anxiety and no guilt.

There was no light flashing before my eyes. My only concern was for my children. 15 seconds later I was placed on an emergency room table – unable to breathe, but aware that my brain and my body were shutting down due to lack of oxygen.

I remember opening my eyes for a moment and seeing two ER physicians standing over me while nurses and paramedics stood at the door. I saw halos around their heads. I thought I was heaven bound.

11 hours later I woke up in the Intensive Care Unit. I thought his was a funny looking heaven. It became apparent to me that I had a large intubation tube down my throat. Thank goodness my hands were locked in place because had they not been, I would have pulled that intubation tube right out of my throat. I squirmed in my bed. I was alive.

Two hours later a physician came into the room and told me I had been dead on arrival. "You are very lucky to be alive."

It is important for me to remember this near-death experience and to share the experience with you. Today, I can truly say that I thought I would surely die. I had an undeniable faith that whatever happened I was in God's hands – good, bad, or indifferent. It was the most divine and blessed experience anyone could have. Absolute faith, no fear.

CHAPTER 1: MEETING SELF

Freedom from Self

We start out as a square peg (negative will), trying to fit into a round hole (reality). Let's look at the banishment of fear, particularly the fear of death. Let us also examine how and when to deal with guilt.

The feeling of being separated from our physical self is bliss without consequences. Sharp awareness of the blueprint to this liberation produces a blending of the senses and a total appreciation of others. To their pain, their joy, their love and feelings of insecurity. To be totally aware of our emotional and intellectual thoughts we must analyze the negative will of self and examine our current view of reality.

The guilt and the fear that precedes unresolved guilt is simply fear within self. There is a key to unlock each individual guilt and emotion associated with guilt feelings: including encounters and resentment of others, situations, or even unresolved financial problems. Basically, every overwhelming hidden part, or past emotional guilt, must be defined and dissected. We must take a close look at each and every portion, pinpointing the occurrences and scenarios, asking ourselves what we are going to do about dealing with them. Some people will react in a way as to say, "I am going to get them back," or "I am going to show them how much they hurt me."

Self-Assessment Dissection.

1. Feeling
2. Hearing
3. Judgement
4. Touch
5. Ambiguity
6. Connection

HEARING

- » I am sensitive.
- » I listen to direction.
- » I can distinguish change for the best.
- » I enjoy silence.
- » I am attuned to subtle changes and inflections of negativity.

JUDGEMENT

- » I make judgments based on time and research.
- » I am not required to cast judgment upon people.
- » I can reliably judge the quality of people.
- » I am not to take myself too seriously.

TOUCH

- » I am aware of the feel of the surface that surrounds me daily.
- » I am sensitive to the quality of the overall fabric of materials.
- » My friends say I give great hugs.
- » I know how to listen with my hands.
- » When I touch someone, I can tell if he or she is tense or relaxed.

AMBIGUITY

- » I am comfortable not knowing all there is to know in life.
- » I am attuned to the rhythms of my intuition.
- » I can handle change.
- » I see the humor in life.
- » I know when I am feeling anxious.
- » I spend sufficient enjoyable time on my own.
- » I delight in paradox and I am sensitive to irony.
- » I appreciate the importance of conflict in inspiring creativity.

CONNECTION

» I try to experience a sense of connectedness with all creation.
» My life goals and priorities are formulated clearly and integrated with my own values and objectives of purpose.
» I am working hard to articulate the patterns, connections and networks in my family, workplace, and recreation activities.
» I have a well-developed sense of proportion.
» I seek a holistic approach to diet, health and healing.
» I enjoy similarities, analogies and metaphors.
» I am ecologically aware.

CHAPTER 2: KARMIC RELATIONSHIP

It seems that individuals are drawn together or attracted to each other until they have a harmonious relationship, or a more manipulated or forced relationship.

If we harbor inner hurts, hates, or resentments towards another person, it is because we see ourselves in that other person. Until we resolve our own bad behaviors, we will continuously be bothered by people who have those same bad behaviors. And we won't even know why.

Karma can be defined as such: an individual's behavior dictates what happens to them because of said behavior. We directly and indirectly cause the results of our actions to happen. We are responsible for our actions and the outcomes of those actions. Our feelings toward another person are determined by our own behaviors. This karmic relationship does not conflict with the statement that "Karma is only a creative force." Are not both cause and effect created by God, or some unseen force? We create our own problems, thereby causing our reality. But our creativity is a two-edged sword. We can be extremely destructive, or valuably productive.

FIGURE 1

Blueprint to Healing Self

Heart and Soul of Self

In keeping with the law of creative forces, there is a developing resolve to promote a law of bad karma; which is of itself, self-aggrandizing and self-indulgent. Both are retarding.

In this way some think that karma is created and therefore meeting people that fulfil karma is the law. Isn't it said that we reap what we sow?

But our personal losses, being ever present, are interpreted by our past. There exists within the self, 'precedent laws' created by our individual judgments. They are shaped and molded by our moral perceptions. In this book, I provide an analysis of atonement, or atonement with the creative forces, providing you with a way to restore your 'self' to a better condition – that of redemption.

Atonement is defined as follows: 1) reparation given for wrongdoing or injury, 2) amends expiation, 3) the redemption of mankind.

There must be the ability within the heart and the soul to look squarely at, and to understand self. To look 'self' in the face, we must truly know if we are failing in our attempt to be near to God – the universal creative force. If we live in the sincerity of truth within ourselves, we never fool ourselves. We have made our present and we are constantly making our future. Today is the result of yesterday. Tomorrow is the result of today.

Thought with Feelings

Self-perception and judgment are two of the three major forms of experience. The third is 'thought.'

Thought includes remembering, recognizing, abstracting, reasoning, reflecting, associating, imagining, dreaming and the like. If one employs only a few of the types of thought mentioned, then they are sure to neglect what is truly important. If one employs many types of thought processes, then there is a likelihood that they overlap and merge.

We will acquire karma as we meet self in our many attitudes and emotions. When we act with lovingkindness, exhibit patience, or hold onto malicious thoughts. We shape our perceptions and feelings. As a result, we learn that what we do to our fellow man, we also do to ourselves.

With the problem identified, a clear definition of karma can be defined by a clear-cut pattern of behavior. Our karma, the cause-and-effect of our behavior is a problem within self.

We are so absorbed with self that we fail to be considerate of others. We simply ignore the other person's needs, desires, comforts and often become highly judgmental of that person.

We feel that we are treated unjustly. We think we deserve better things. But we can only reap what we have sown. We must meet in the physical reality, what we have done or thought, in the mental.

FIGURE 2

Circle of Karma

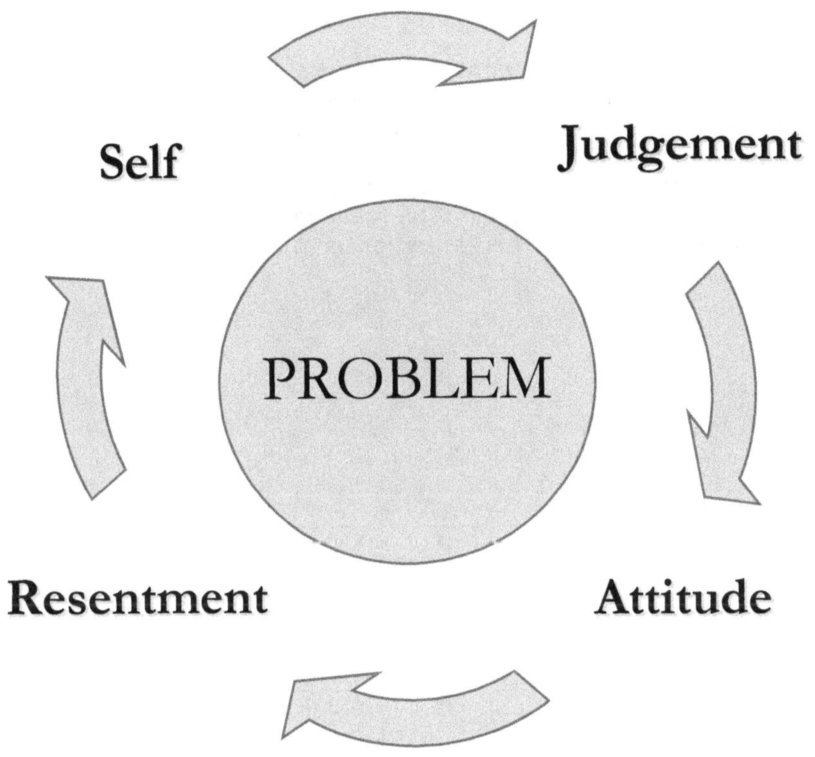

Karmic Influences

Most individuals, in the present, misinterpreted karmic influence. What is karmic influence? Karmic influences are the result that we intuitively receive after having had a karmic experience. Karmic influences are received in the present. This means that we can change future karmic influences.

Each soul should gain the proper concept of destiny. Our destiny is a product of our faith. Destiny is a gift from the creative forces.

Karmic influence is within all of us. When opportunities are presented, it is the entity's 'will' that must be exercised. To enrich our lives, we must eliminate anything that separates us from the creative influences of the higher spiritual forces. Then, in every contact with a higher spiritual force there will be an opportunity for our soul to be fulfilled and thereby meet self. The creative forces will then cause us to embrace that which is necessary for us to enter into the at-oneness with them.

FIGURE 3

KARMIC – SOUL EXPERIENCE

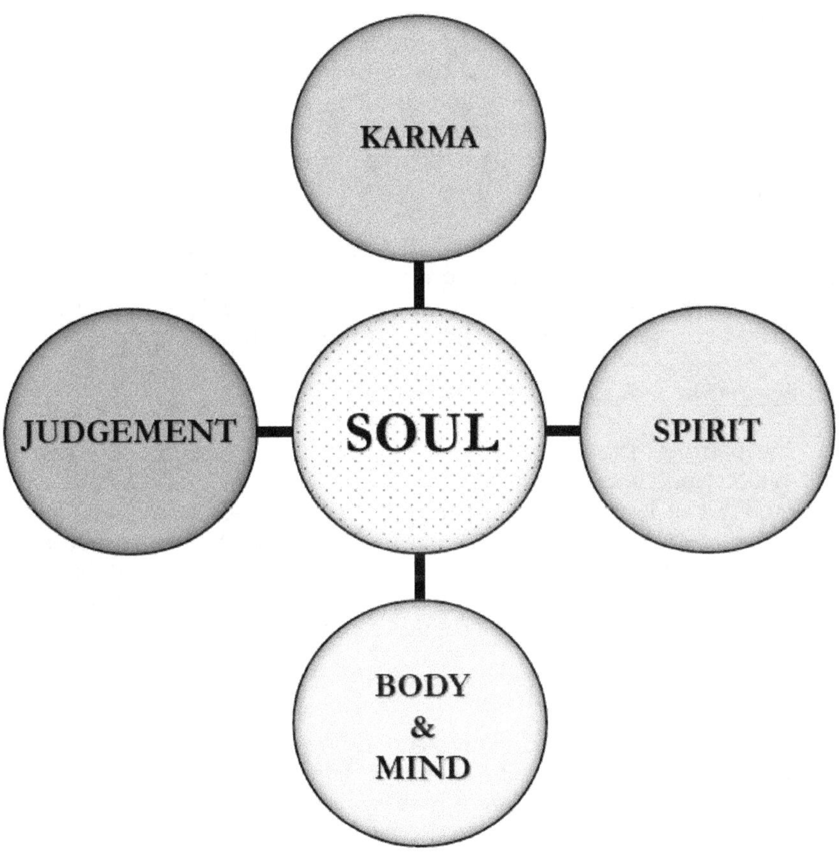

Karmic Forces – Thought and Emotion

Through karmic forces, specifically thought and emotion, a person will come to know a haven of peace and harmony, allowing for stillness and quiet. This stillness and quiet gives way to a final and clear understanding in the belief (and faith) in a higher spiritual force.

Karma – Present and Past

The ramifications associated with karma continuously take us back into the past and reach into the future, if adverse conditions or problems have not been resolved. The judgment stored in our subconscious minds affect our actions. Our thoughts bring on karmic actions and effects. For thought precedes the deed, and thoughts are real things.

From the abundance of the heart the mouth speaks. Thoughts are deeds, and each one builds glorification, edification, or resentment within self. We should then act in the way that is befitting – that which 'fits' and becomes naturally responsive to our individual nature.

Relationship and Creative Forces

The patterns that have been set as markers along man's progress are plain. None mount higher than that which has been left by Him who made the intercession for man so that man, through Him, might have advocacy with the higher power. Those truths and assurances that have been set in Him are true. These can be the experience of every soul. We can become spiritually connected by becoming a pursuer of spirituality and the creative force.

Souls Expressions

There is a passage of expression for the soul through past and present experiences. It is designed to allow for additional altruistic opportunities of expression; that which justifies man in his relationships with one another in mercy, love, patience, suffering, guilt and brotherly love.

We and we alone, are responsible for what we are, as well as our condition on this earth. When we look back, we realize that the things which came to us when we put ourselves in God's hands, were better than anything we could have planned.

Pain and Progress

Years ago, I used to agree with people who suffer. Now, I do not agree except for the ones who suffer in ignorance – who do not understand the purpose and ultimate utility of pain. One must try not to believe in anyone too deeply. Hold your face up to the light even though, for the moment, you do not see.

Three-dimensional

The three dimensions – body-mind-soul of God's grace is *for* you. We live in a three-dimensional world. Body-mind-soul are the three phases that represent the three spiritual attributes that are comprehensible in the material world. With greater intensity, our mental and spiritual faculties become expressed and controlled through the experiences we encounter. These repeated expressions become lifelong judgments. There is no urgency in the material reality for a soul (and mind) to choose its path.

Each soul enters the material environment of others in a particular sphere of activity. Each soul enters the real-world experience for a purpose. Their purpose may not be selfish in nature, though they are very personal in their application and practice.

Each soul continually meets itself in what is called both karma and karmic influence. Remember that life is God. That which constructively grows is fruitful, but that which is destructive deteriorates.

CHAPTER 3: JOURNEY OF KNOWLEDGE

The Network

Though notions like the soul (or ego) help fill some of the space which seems to be missing in our conception of self, it is important to recognize specific faculties that impede spiritual growth; such as memory and judgment. It is just as important to recognize faculties that are conducive to spiritual growth; like imagination. The part of the brain most associated with visual perceptions is also the part most active in imaginative visualization.

Where the brain is concerned it makes no difference whether one is seeing something with the physical eye or with the mind's eye; which I choose to call the spirit connection. The imaginative visualization within the mind's eye uses lifelong subjective experiences which are personal, private and sometimes emotionally painful.

Built-in Limitation of the Mind

We just do not get it. We are unable to understand how judgment acts within the subconscience. The state of consciousness means to be awake and aware of one's perception and reality, which is objective, versus our past judgment and decision making, which is subjective. The outcome of such thinking brings about traditional good and bad thoughts. Now, how do we deal with feelings?

With knowledge, specific information and clear perception, comes freedom from the delusional state of mind. Close attention should be paid to understanding what constitutes knowledge.

It can be difficult to draw a clear distinction between true understanding and false understanding. Once a clear distinction is made, we will know where to focus our attention. The application of attention requires a great deal of effort. Our purpose is to practice focusing our attention until it becomes second nature. Over time you will learn to make a clear distinction between true understanding and false understanding. In other words, you will find freedom from a delusional state of mind.

FIGURE 4

Built-in Limitation of the Mind

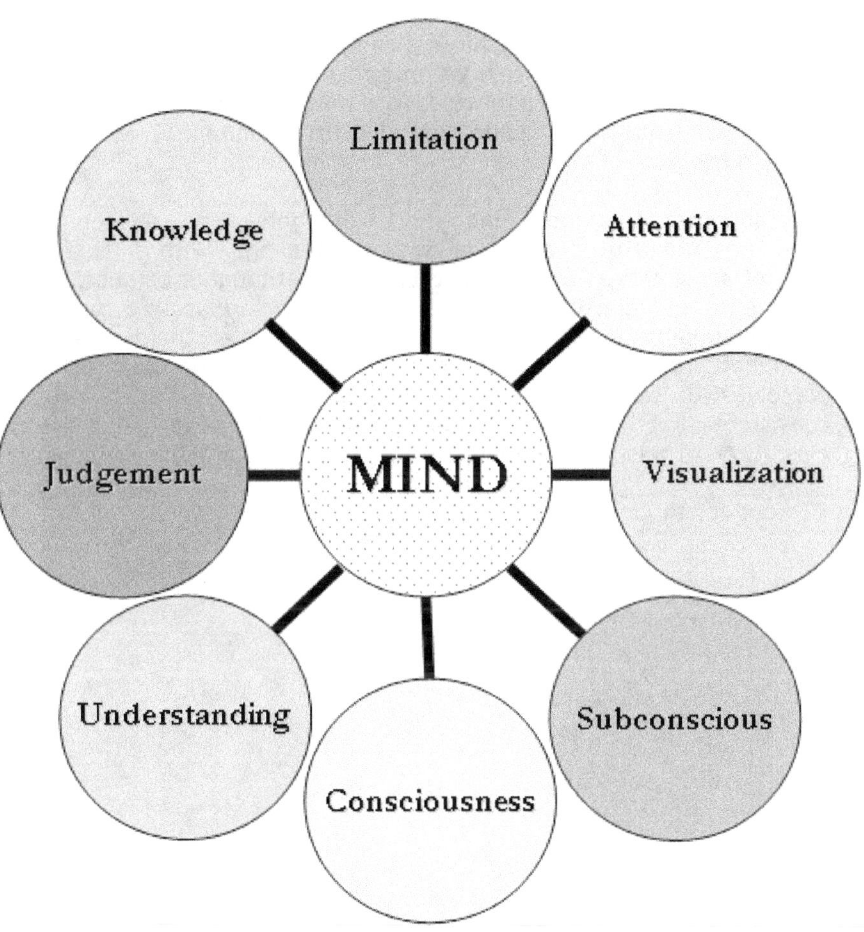

Through the journey into self-introspection, we are trying to discipline our mental processes. This is known as concentration. We should hope and want to practice the development of our attention span into a laser focused concentration, otherwise known as 'meditation.'

Training our Attention Span

Choose any kind of object, shape or image that can be held in the hand or in the mind's eye for a good length of time.

Training the attention span is closely linked with learning how to control our mental processes. We must find a quiet physical space and clear the mind for a peaceful release within our 'self.' We will learn to calm down from the outside, in. This is fundamental to our total thinking process.

Thoughts, thoughts, and more thoughts. The subconscience constantly talks to us with emotions and feelings. With a heightened level of sensitivity, we feel and then release thoughts of guilt, anger, judgment, revenge, care and sorrow from our minds. We internalize and personalize every emotion. And then we let them evaporate. Thoughts are almost impossible to stop. Therefore, we must train ourselves to trust our instinct and train those instincts with the consistent practice of meditation, constant discipline, analysis and insight. All of this is the food of knowledge for the mind.

Food for thought!

FIGURE 5

Connecting Focus Time Within Self

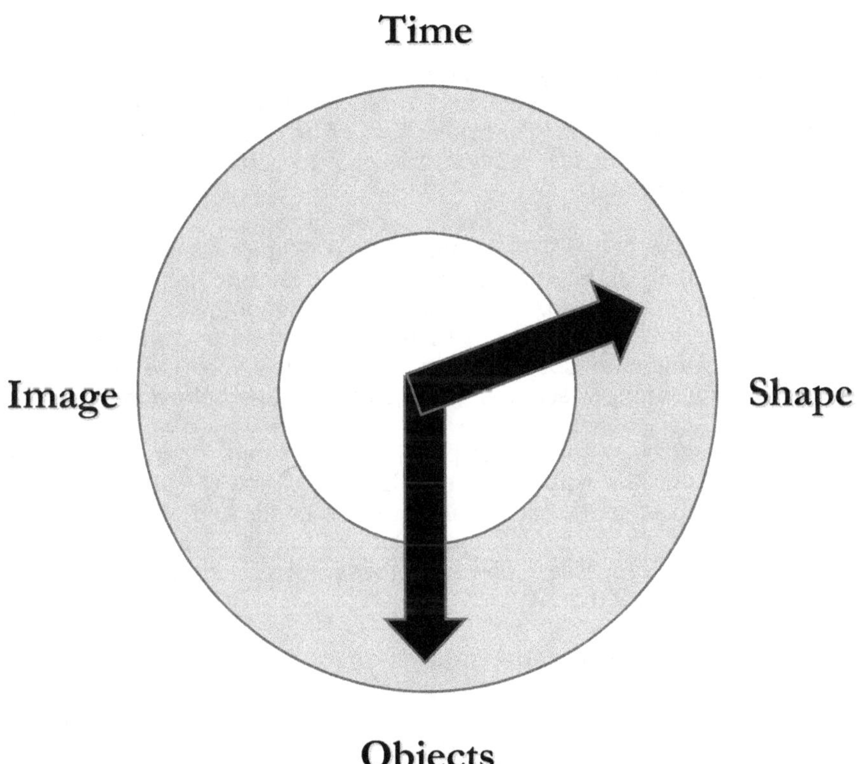

Analysis in Attention

The combination of analysis and concentration will help your attention span, which in turn helps with meditation. Because it is an individualized experience, it is best to learn what meditation process works best for you. Meditative practices provide a settled and disciplined state of mind. If the aim is to dwell deeper into ever present (specific) thoughts, it is not enough to simply have a focused mind. This is where the two disciplines become a great aid.

Discipline

Discipline is a method of training that gives us the ability to perform in a calm and tranquil way. We must acquire the skill of letting go – and following the direction of observation. The goal is to gain more knowledge by practicing tranquil training while holding your focus without distraction. That takes lots of practice and patience. But it is a great method which provides the door to better understanding of how we think and feel.

Dalai Lama's book "The Universe in a Single Atom" provides a detailed account of how both tranquil abiding and insight may be systematically cultivated. Combining the thoughts of long-lasting tranquility and clear perception, then applying it to one's life leads to the understanding of specific aspects of reality – to the point that one's understanding affects thoughts, emotions and behaviors.

There must be a specific emphasis on the need for maintaining a fine equilibrium. The equilibrium should be between the single pointed concentrated placement of the mind on one hand, and the application of a focused beam of analysis on the other. Our mind wants to create different mental processes; however, these processes have a potential to undermine each other.

Single pointed concentration allows you to focus on a chosen object, holding the mind on an object with little distraction. Thoughts move from one aspect of the object to another while we are cultivating insight. There is a point where full fusion of insight requires directed action. It is advised that you begin this experiment with as much sharpness into inquiry as possible. The objective is to try to hold the mind singularly and pointedly on the resulting insight for as long as possible.

When we began to lose the force of the insight, I advise re-commencing the analytic process. Regroup – start over with a clear mind. This may lead to a higher level of mental capability at which both analysis and focus can, in some way, begin to become effortless.

We are analyzing the transient nature core – that essential part of our own existence. We can and will, in time, understand this intellectually. We do not behave as though we have integrated the core awareness. Rather, we are working toward the concentration on this topic, to bring the insight to life so that we begin to appreciate the preciousness of every moment of our existence on earth.

Force of Thought

For everything that happens in the objective world, there must be something in the subjective world which perfectly balances it. Thought is an actual working power. Otherwise, there would be nothing by which the universe could be governed. Most of the inner processes of our thought have been subconscious. But when we understand the law, we learn to consciously embody what we wish for. Think only of the wish, and we are drawn silently toward it.

Individuality and Thought

We cannot live a choice-less life. Every day, every moment, every second there is a choice. If this were not so, we would not be individuals. We have the right to choose that which we wish to experience. We have the right to associate. We have a say-so in the house and city we want to live in. We are individuals, and the only way we can be individuals is to be spontaneous. We have the right to choose what we shall induce in our minds.

Cause and affect are really one. And if we have given cause, we set in motion an equal effect.

> There is one infinite principle, one infinite thought, one infinite creative power, but countless number of forms. One totally connected

God and You

> Awaken to the principal fact that we are one in nature with God or we shall not find this new life

CHAPTER 4: MEDITATION

Effortless Meditation

To begin, we become aware of the body and the breath. In a state of calm, we cultivate awareness of the very subtle changes that occur in the body during the period of 'pre-practice,' even between the in-breath and out-breath. This is the start of the 'awareness arising state' where nothing within our existence stays static or unchanging. Once we know this very important fact, we enter the 'effortless process.'

FIGURE 6

Meditation Practice Scale

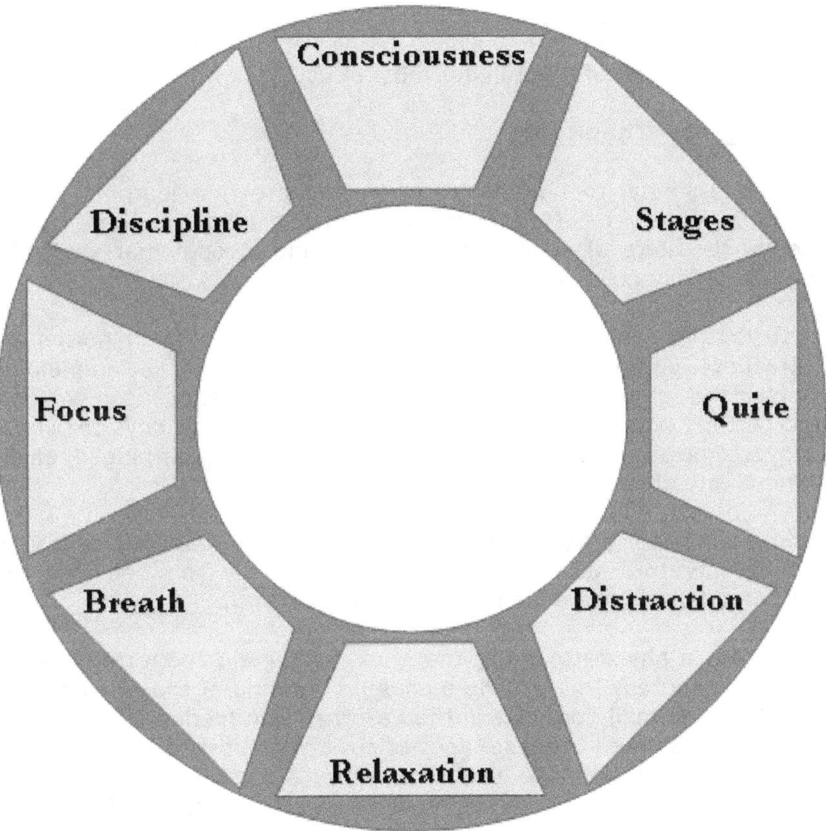

Preparing for Relaxation and Meditation

Three starting points are required to begin your journey into the meditation state.

A. A quiet and safe place where you will not be disturbed.
B. A bed, chair or couch on which to relax.
C. The willingness to alter your consciousness.

The goal is to create an environment of solitude. Worrying about being intruded upon is not conducive to proper relaxation. The idea of wondering if someone will intrude upon your quiet environment is enough to keep you from having success in meditation. Our mental blocks are enough of a hurdle for most of us.

Quiet Place – Thank You

It is essential to have quiet when you are first learning to use meditation practices. Meditation is a practice based on successfully altering the state of your consciousness. Find a room that works for you – hopefully noise free.

If you are sensitive to sound and find that even minor noises are distracting, you can ease some of your frustration by reminding yourself that as you get better at altering your consciousness, you will also become better at shutting out the evidence of the physical world. To overcome sound distraction, try using commercial earplugs – easily found in any drugstore.

You will need to keep your body warm. As you start relaxing, your body temperature will decrease. To keep your body from becoming too cold, grab your favorite blanket and lay it over you.

Choose a physical posture that you can remain comfortable in for 30 to 60 minutes. This usually means no crossing of the arms or legs unless you normally practice in the Eastern Asian meditative traditions and are accustomed to these types of positions. Crossed arms and legs become uncomfortable for most of us. After a short while this physical discomfort will distract from the focus you are trying to maintain.

If you choose to sit, it is usually recommended by the advanced practitioners that you attempt to keep your spine as straight as possible, to keep the energy flowing throughout your body and to prevent stress point fatigue from causing discomfort which can distract you.

If you choose to lie down, make sure you began practicing at least 10 minutes at a time. Any more than 10 minutes and it is certain that you will inadvertently fall asleep.

Maintain an awareness of physical location. This controlling action separates thoughts from dreams and other uncontrolled psychic experiences.

Eastern Mystic School of Thought

East Asian and Indian practitioners have a whole catalog of interesting meditative postures. Most of which, Westerners find hard to either achieve or maintain. These often involve contorting the arms and legs into positions that people conditioned to sitting in hardback chairs or plush sofas are not accustomed to. The eastern spiritual schools also teach that various positions are best for different types of meditation. If you are already using one or more of these various positions, you are free to select the one that you think will work best for you. Choosing a posture that is familiar and comfortable is best when beginning to learn 'surrender' meditation.

Altered States of Consciousness

Success in meditation does not require a deep meditative state, or what is sometimes called an altered state of consciousness. But it does require that you know how to enter and exit a state with reasonable ease and comfort.

Despite what people tell you about meditation, there is no great mystery to this process. There is no inherent danger, nor is it something that only the talented can achieve. The word 'altered' merely means 'changed.' An altered state of consciousness refers only to a variation in the number of brainwave cycles your brain produces per second.

This is not new-age psychobabble, but a measurement taken by an actual machine known as an electroencephalogram or EEG. These changes in brain activity are divided into four categories: Beta, Alpha, Theta, and Delta.

Beta

Awake – Beta is the normal waking consciousness used while actively thinking, studying, reasoning and conversing.

Alpha

The light to medium altered state – Alpha is used for light meditation. Alpha is also the mental state needed to succeed at most spiritual endeavors, including astral projection of the mind.

The Alpha state also underlies daydreaming, focused non-analytical thought, watching television, light reading, REM (rapid eye movement) dream sleep, and sleep walking.

Theta

Deep altered state, Theta, is associated with Zen and other complex spiritual practices. Waking from this mid-to-deep sleep level can be moderately difficult or unpleasant.

Delta

Point to consider – the Delta level characterizes the very deepest level of sleep and is present when we are in a coma. At this level, there is no awareness of the physical body or its needs. Although, some people can recall details about events and conversations that have taken place in the room around them. Waking from this state ranges from very difficult to almost impossible.

FIGURE 7

Characteristics of Sleep Awareness of the Physical Body

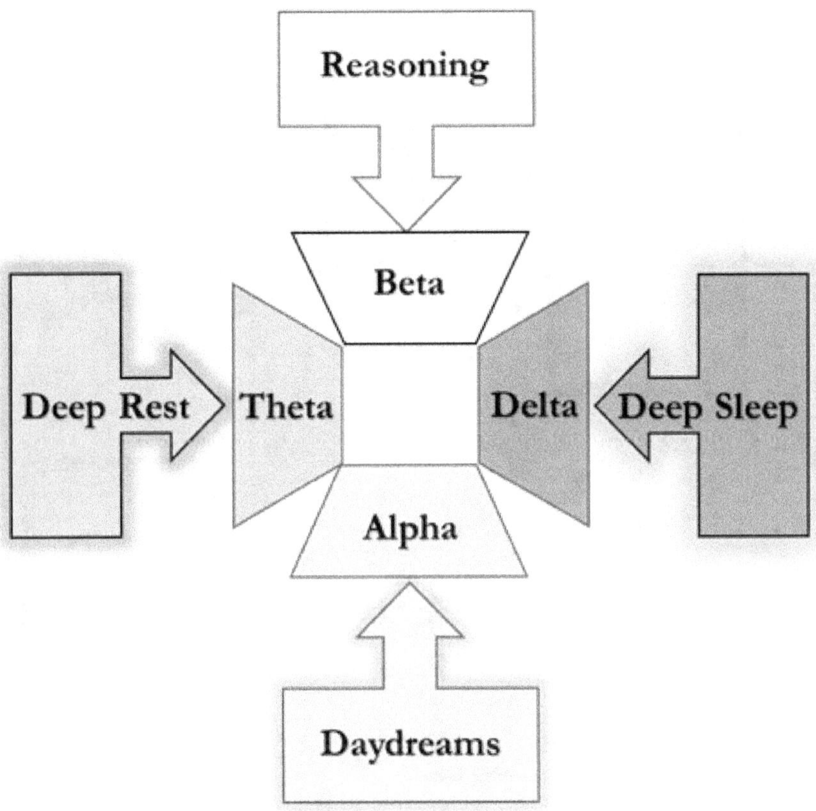

FIGURE 8

Activity Level Heart Brain Divided into 4 Categories

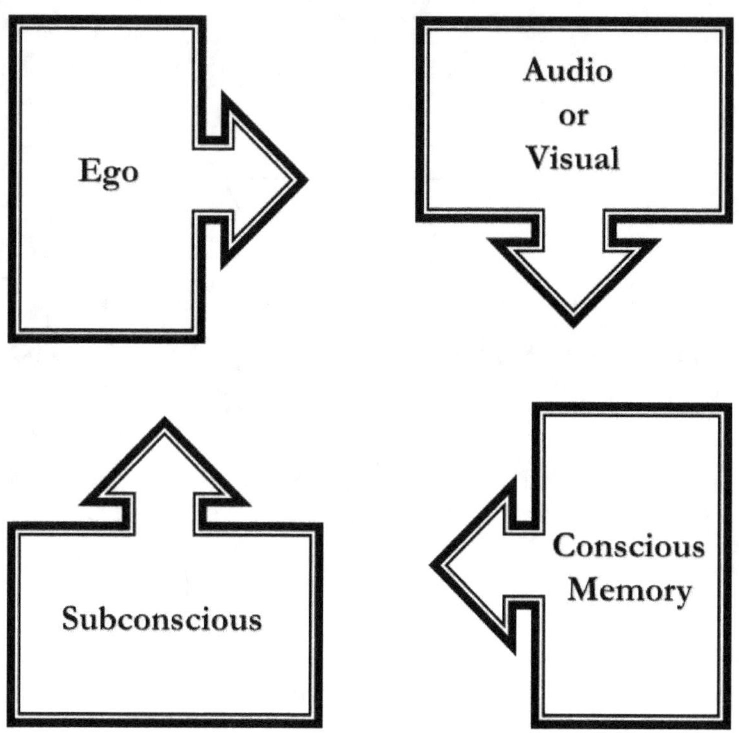

Learning the Art of Meditation

People who meditate on a regular basis acquire a host of other benefits. Studies have proven that meditation lowers blood pressure, helps build strong immune systems, decreases susceptibility to stress related illnesses and produces more restful sleep. Our thinking becomes quicker. And compared to those who do not meditate, energy levels are increased. The art of meditation will open and enhance all areas of your life, including your spiritual life.

There are numerous books and digital offerings on the market that will help you learn meditation. They include thorough details of meditation and teach how to focus on a particular method. These are great to use if meditation alone is the end goal.

The primary goal is to learn the power and freedom of meditation. This requires only an intermediate skill level that, while still requiring practice, does not require a special library from which to learn.

There is no limit to the power and control one can obtain with the benefits of meditation. Almost everyone can have some success meditating by fully relaxing the body and taking control of all conscious thoughts.

Progressive Method of Relaxation

To begin your meditation practice, use a warm, quiet, private place. Choose a body posture which will allow for relaxation and comfort for at least 30 minutes. As you practice, less time will be required to become comfortable. Find a keyword or mantra. For example, 'Victorious Spirit,' or a symbolic sign to open up your soul. Illustrative examples are shown in figure 9.

As you become comfortable close your eyes and center yourself. Ask for the Victorious Spirit to come into your heart. Take a deep breath and center yourself. Exhale within the rhythm of your heartbeat. Slowly breathe in with the beat of your heart.

At first this will be an unnatural feeling because we have not reached out to the spirit with breath, body, mind and heartbeat. It will take time to adjust your body and mind to this exercise.

FIGURE 9

Symbols of Meditation Focus

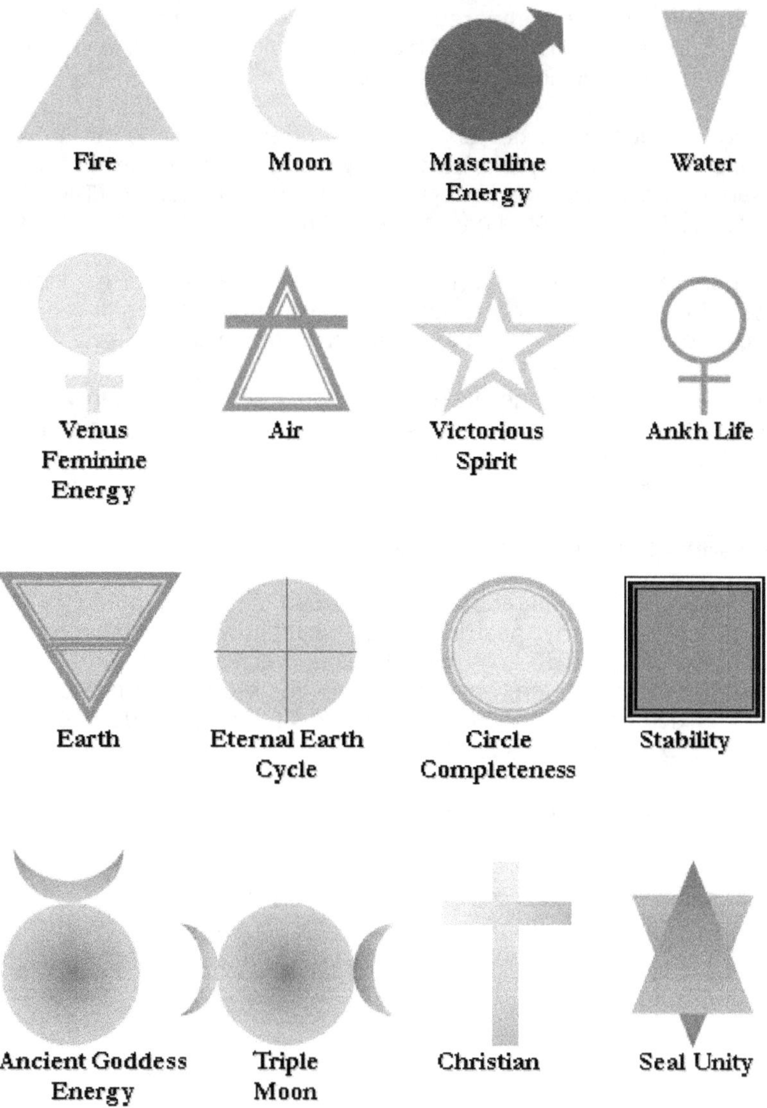

Visualize Release

As you exhale, visualize all the tension draining from your body. There will undoubtedly be some tense spots that remain after you do this. We will come back later and slay these 'worry dragons.' But for now, just relax as much as possible and continue. Next, you want to do what has been called progressive relaxation. Progressive relaxation is a meditative process that allows you to relax your entire body by focusing on its individual points, from heel to head. It is important to relax each point of the body thoroughly before continuing to the next point.

Start with your feet. Let go and take a deep breath. Let in the spirit, allowing it to remove the tension within the bottom of your feet, toes, and continuing up through the ankles, calves, knees and thighs. Then continue up to the stomach, the solar plexus and out into the hands. Extend each finger and let the blood flow out. Then, move up through the heart, the thyroid and into the head, starting at the temples then to the forehead and out the top of the head.

Point of the Body

When each individual point is mentally isolated, its condition becomes clearer, and therefore easier to relax than the whole body at one time. It is a time-consuming process, but as you do it you will become aware of just how many small pockets of tension that you carry around on a regular basis.

Over the years, I have tried all types of meditation programs. I moved on to progressive relaxation. I was frustrated during a season when clinched muscles were always present. And many years later I still find that if I am in pain or emotionally upset, there are areas where I collect tension and where it is hardest to relax. This type of relaxation is also a great technique for helping you to fall asleep, if you're having trouble drifting off due to a stress filled day. This type of relaxation has benefits beyond 'simple release' meditation.

FIGURE 10

Points to Focus on to Relieve Stress

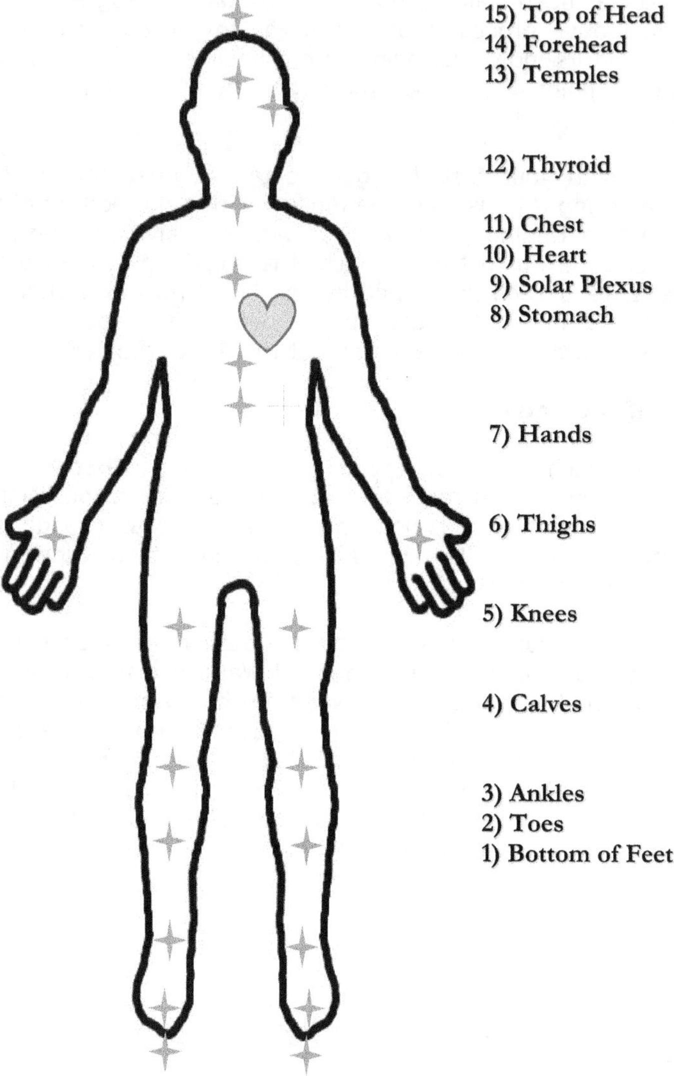

Letting go of all negative energy at these points leads to deeper meditation.

Take five breaths and start letting go.

1. Bottom of the feet
2. Toes
3. Ankles
4. Calf
5. Knees
6. Thighs
7. Hands
8. Stomach
9. Solar Plexus
10. Heart
11. Chest
12. Thyroid
13. Temples
14. Forehead
15. Top of the Head

Focusing Your Spirit

Let us review what is most important. Once you feel fully relaxed, take another deep breath. Begin to focus your thoughts on one thing only. If you tend to be a visually oriented person, then you might want to pick an image or symbol to hold in your mind. Keep the symbol's shape, texture and color simple for now. You can practice by staring at the symbol for several minutes just prior to falling asleep.

Subconscious Practice

Symbols are strong motivators that the subconscious can latch onto and carry you into the dream world, allowing you to forge an even stronger link with them.

The subsequent dreams that you may have about your symbol could offer you special insight into its meaning. Insight that you might miss if you do not choose to engage. It is reported that such dreams have provided the practitioner with a spontaneous relaxation queue, triggered through their chosen symbolic gateway.

Aurally Oriented

If, on the other hand you are somebody that is aurally oriented; who hears ideas rather than seeing them, you might want to pick a phrase to say over and over to yourself. Keep the phrase short and related to your ultimate goal. This will alter your consciousness in the same way that symbols motivate insight. In this instance you might want to repeat something like, "I am relaxing, I am relaxing, let go, let God, let go, let God." Find a phrase that is befitting and positive to you.

Be sure to keep your affirmation positive and in the present tense. In these low or altered states the mind becomes very receptive. This is one reason that the idea of 'sleep learning' has gone through a period of popularity. If you make your statement in the future, you may end up keeping your goal in the future as well.

Make sure you state your phrase as if it is already a fact in your life. And keep it positive. Do not focus on the negatives. To dwell on them only feeds your self-doubt by pulsing negative energy into your practice. If you really want to overcome any negative thoughts that stand in your way, then simply make an affirmation that already sees your success as part of your current reality.

Another reason for this affirmation is to convince all levels of your mind of their truth. We have a sense of the brain-mind-body connection and have some understanding of how we help shape our own reality. Once the mind is convinced of something there is little that can stop the brain and body from following through.

Major Point of the Mind

Holding onto one single thought is not as easy as it sounds. In the beginning, your mind will want to wander off and seek out something more entertaining to consider. This is the point where many people give up in true frustration. We must resist the urge to quit, or even to stop and tell ourselves we will start again next Monday. This only lets that resistant part of your mind win the battle. And like a spoiled child, it will only cry all the louder the next time you want it to do something it doesn't like, until you give into it again. This starts you on a downward spiral of failure that can be hard to overcome when you finally figure out where you went wrong.

Whenever your mind wanders away from your goal, just put it back on the thought you wanted to have and continue as if nothing had happened.

Slowly work your way to where you can hold a single thought for at least five minutes. Keep in mind that you will be unaware of the passage of time while meditating. So, remember to look at the clock just before you start and just after each session to check your progress.

Mastering the Experience

Mastering this part of the meditation art may only take a few weeks or a few months depending on your surrender experience and your efforts. The next step is getting into your meditative state and allowing a dramatic scene to form in your relaxed mind. Remember to let go, find the scenario you find irresistible and let it unfold naturally, in front of your inner eyes, as if it were being projected onto a 360-degree movie screen.

Virtual Reality

This is your time to enter the best virtual reality there is. A chance to live out your greatest desire. There are no rules or limitations. Make yourself the main star, writer, and director. Remember to allow God to help you with the process. The sensation you will experience while meditating and often the mere practice of seeing yourself in the scene, will actually place you there. So, take off and totally relax within your inner self.

Mental Counting

Mental Counting is another method of achieving and deepening an altered state. It can be as simple as counting forward and then counting backwards. Talking to the mind is similar to counting sheep to overcome insomnia.

Mental counting helps many people relax and achieve a receptive state of mind. The numbers you choose to begin with, and end with, are up to you. Mental counting can be combined with your controlled breathing if this helps you focus. You can also repeat a set of numbers over and over again to yourself. If, for instance, you are part of a spiritual tradition that treats seven as a sacred number, as many Christian mystic schools do, or even if it is just your personal lucky number based on experience in numerology, then you might want to count down from seven to one, over and over, to enter your meditation, and up from one to seven to exit.

Power Breathing

One of the most basic of all meditative practices is controlled breathing. This is a skill elevated to a high spiritual art in Eastern Asia. To mimic this, you will need to allow the natural rhythm of your breathing to lull you into a deeper altered state as you meditate.

As you follow these rhythmic steps, you begin to rediscover increased mental stimulation and other health benefits brought about by proper breathing. This discovery is primarily based upon the probability that a few smart folks have found a way to make it profitable.

In trendy Los Angeles, you can now go to oxygen bars to breathe clean air as you discuss your latest corporate raid. Professional athletes are rushing to hire breathing coaches whom they feel will show them the secrets to getting the top performance from their bodies by altering the way they breathe. There is also interest in reading books published by holistic fitness gurus.

Breathing Technique

Breathing correctly is essential for complete and thorough meditation. Newcomers to altered state work impede their own progress by not taking breath control into account. The concept sounds silly to many people who think that proper breathing comes naturally – that no one should have to be taught, but this is not true. Healthy breathing is natural deep breathing that comes from the diaphragm and not from the chest.

The diaphragm is an elongated muscle situated below the lungs like the surface of a drum. It is responsible for expanding and contracting them. When you breathe deep, it is the diaphragm muscle which is moving air, not the lungs themselves.

Look at the way you breathe. Does your diaphragm move? Or is your breathing shallow and centered in the upper part of the chest? Now take a few slow deep breaths. Is your midsection, your diaphragm, doing most of the expanding and contracting? Or, are you forcing this task on your chest?

Consider the position of your shoulders when you are standing or sitting. If your shoulders rise and fall with each breath you take, you are doing something wrong. The shoulders should remain perfectly still as you breathe.

Most students of meditation can be taught to breathe correctly if they are lying down flat on their back. If you are unsure if you are breathing from your diaphragm, try lying on the floor and concentrating on your natural breathing. Notice how your stomach area, not your chest, has a natural tendency to rise and fall.

Sleeping and Breathing

People breathe right while they are sleeping. Everyone breathes correctly during sleep unless an illness or other physical problem causes interference. Take some time to watch a sleeper breathe. Notice how they take slow deep breaths of air from the solar plexus area and not from the chest.

Professional singers also know how to breathe correctly, since diaphragm breathing is essential for controlling the phrasing of songs and producing powerful voices. If you are trying to center yourself while meditating and find that your mind still tends to wander, you may want to try counting each breath as it comes to you. Try this on both the exhale and then on the inhale, to see if it makes a difference in the way you feel.

It is standard practice to inhale through your nose and exhale through your mouth, when doing deliberate deep breathing exercises.

Pledge of Intention

It is of great importance to set your goals high and to work towards a powerful and stabilizing meditative awareness. Before entering the last state of higher meditation, one must have a deliberate intention not to allow the meditation to be distracted by recollections of past experiences, or by hopes or fears of future events. The anticipation of such events is sometimes harmful and can cause a major distraction in the conscious mind.

How can one come to make a silent pledge during this necessary step of meditation? How can we work through the meditation process without being seduced by thoughts of the past or the future? Can we really remain fully focused on awareness of the present? These questions are critical, because in our everyday normal states we tend to be tied either to recollections of the past or to hopes and fears about the future. We tend to live either in the past or in the future, and rarely are we fully in the present.

When one is in meditation it may be helpful to face a wall that has no contrasting colors or patterns that might distract one's attention. A cream, muted color is more restful. Always observe the mind resting naturally in its own state. As one begins, one will notice that all sorts of thoughts arise in the mind, like bumper-to-bumper traffic. One should allow whatever thoughts arise to do so freely, regardless of whether one perceives them as wholesome or unwholesome. Do not reinforce them, repress them or turn to evaluate them in judgment. Any of these responses will create future proliferation of thoughts and provide the fuel that keeps the chain reaction going. One must simply observe the thought then "let go and let God." When one does this – just as steam rises and dissolves into the air, the distractive thought processes simply arise and dissolve within the mind.

Leaving the Meditative State

When you are ready to conclude your session of meditation, simply begin to get a sense of your physical body once more. Do this by taking the focus off your meditation and turning it on to your physical body. Begin to think about your head, your face, your neck, etc. And remember that inner feeling you have obtained in the process.

It is also recommended that you try, whenever possible, to come out of the meditative state using the same process by which you entered. This keeps your analytical mind, which always craves logic, happy. Thus, keeping it in sync with your creative mind. Doing so allows for a smooth transition of thought and mental images. When you feel solidly back in the physical, you may open your eyes and begin to move your body.

You can do something physical like stretching. This will help clear the separation between the meditative world and the physical world. Get your blood moving and your heart pounding. This is the time to revel in the fact that you are alive and fully a part of the physical world.

Creative Visualization

Creative visualization is the practice of mentally envisioning a desired outcome and infusing it with personal feelings of energy and harmony. And then releasing it to the cosmos (our spirit-will) so that it can grow to manifest in the physical world. While all that sounds unduly complicated, what it boils down to is that creative visualization transfers a 'thought form' into the physical world.

The terms creative visualization and positive thinking are sometimes used interchangeably, depending on the spiritual orientation of the one doing the visualizing. In both cases the goal is to take a desired need and bring it into being. Both terms refer to more than just thinking about a desired idea and its result. This process seeks to attain that idea and its results, by efforts made in both the seen and unseen worlds.

Creative visualization is easy. Though I have had many people tell me that they cannot do it. Their insistence that this skill is beyond them is probably due to misconceptions about the process. Too many people make it harder than it really is.

Creative visualization is mental vision. We visualize each time we daydream, work out a project in our heads, create a new decorating scheme for our surroundings, or make plans for positive aspects in all areas of our lives. Anytime you think about something and see it happening, you are using creative visualization. What differentiates it as creative visualization is the level at which you control the process, while using the spirit's energy to make it a reality.

CHAPTER 5: CHANNELING

Channels of Energy

We live our lives as channels of energy. Every day we exercise this state. We make choices about how to channel the life forces into actions. We work, play, keep house, and interact with our friends and associates. We amuse ourselves and deal with emergencies. There is nothing particularly mysterious about acting in a manner that allows us to become channels in everyday life. At least not on the surface.

There are three components involved in being the channel that we call a human being; the input, the output, and the medium between the two. The input side of energy comes from being alive. The air we breathe, the food we eat are both a given. By using the word 'given,' we point out an important fact. The inputted energy is not ours to own because it belongs to life itself. But it is ours to use – to channel.

The output side of energy are the experiences we make for ourselves, our actions or behaviors. In doing these things, we channel life energy into our physical body and turn it into thoughts and actions.

The medium between the input and the output is the psychology of the mind. Within this psychology are valuable and worthwhile ideas about how to expand our energy, and the contemplated choices associated with those ideas.

We try to exercise our will by using the mind. We regulate incoming energy and force it toward our choice of outgoing activity. As simple, and familiar as the image of a channel may be, it will nevertheless point to creativity that is basic to our lives. The mystery of life creates us as flesh and blood. In response, we create our human lives and touch the lives of those around us.

Truth Manifesting

For truth shall indeed make you free. Free, even though you are bound by the chains of errors and consequences that result from the errors in your own experiences.

Freedom then, is the first spiritual approach or the attitude that one should seek to achieve. Running on a spiritual path towards freedom is helpful, and it is easily attainable in nature. So often it has been shown that each soul manifesting on the earth is the result of that soul's use of opportunities in its relationship to God the Father.

Let us consider that there is a 'body emotion,' a 'mind emotion,' and a 'soul emotion'. The soul is spirit. The mind may have its 'high or low pressures' in thought. The body, although individualized, is physical and of the earth. As an earthly entity, the body was first created from that which was of the earth. Therefore, those earthly elements meet their own receptors in the blood supply, producing growth and rejuvenation.

Free Will – Self

Free will is a developmental factor which a person chooses, or a belief system that gives us the ability to experience freedom of choice. Free will gives us an internal sense of being free. Free to choose different courses of action in life. Knowing the truth about free will is pertinent in various experiences, whether in thought or in deed.

I believe that thoughts *are* deeds. Present thoughts are wholly based on past influences learned through individual experiences. Our past judgments have completely taken the place of our emotional state of consciousness.

As each of us enters a material plane of reality (on reality's terms), we bring with us a basic need for fulfilling our life's purpose. And we need to understand that most of what we experience in the material plane is man-made. All the *material* wants, and desires create a gap which impedes the soul from becoming one with the creative forces.

Becoming one with the creative forces allows us to reach a higher level of intuitive thought. It is necessary to override the desire for material gains. Self-indulgence, self-gratification and self-exaltation clog the channel between the creative force input, and the true freedom of a positive Godly output. In truth, it is harder to achieve absolute freedom than free will. Eliminating self with just one attempt, one inspiring book or one prayer is highly unlikely.

Fear is perhaps the most devastating of all emotions. Fear often stems from past experiences which are buried deep inside us. Some of those fears seem foolish and inexplicable in the present. But they fulfilled a very valid and real purpose in the past.

Creation – Channel – Surrender

A river is a source of energy that the human mind can visualize and mentally consider. Channeling the energy from that flowing river and turning it into a dynamic force of energy to produce electricity, capable of grinding grain or sawing lumber, is also very conceivable.

The nucleus of an atom is held together by unfathomable energies. Depending upon the state, and release of energy, we can generate enough electricity to power a metropolitan area or cause a great explosion which could potentially destroy a piece of the world. Einstein's formula for Special Relativity states that Energy is equal to Mass times the Speed of Light squared, or E=MC squared. The energy bound up in matter is equivalent to the mass of that matter being accelerated to the speed of light, in an instant. The energy released from one gram of salt would vaporize your house and demolish your entire neighborhood.

Energy is bound potential. When balanced, it is a neutral force. How the energy is channeled determines its effects. It is channeled according to the blueprint by which the energy is applied.

FIGURE 11

Energy Within Space Time and Earth

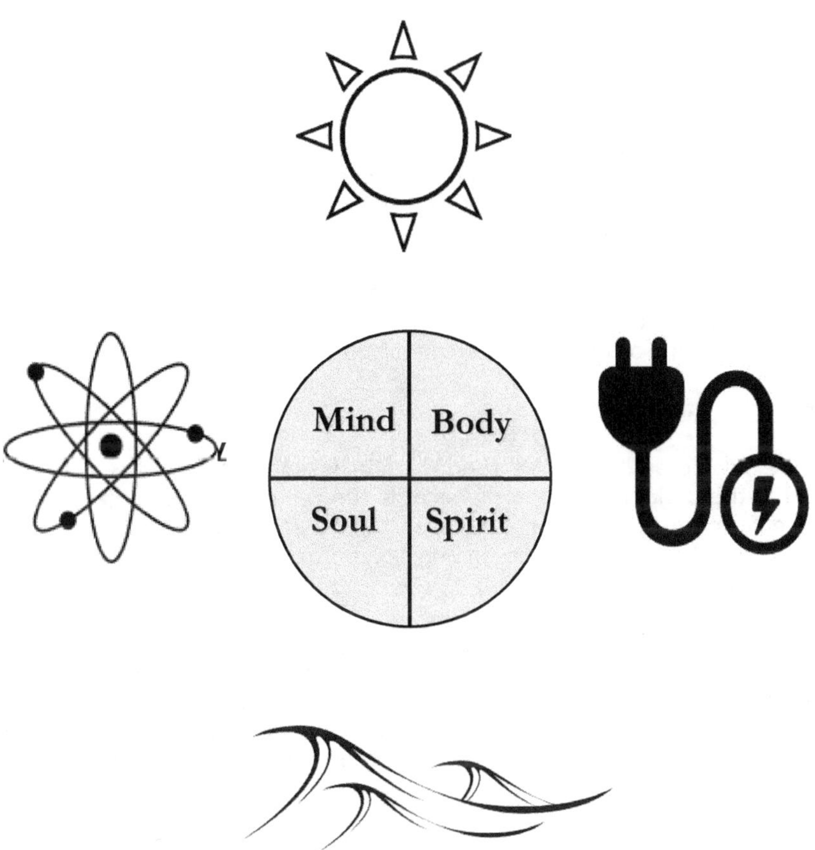

God's love and Spirit are the ultimate forces in the universe. They are the essential and basic energy of creation. There are no other sources of energy that can manifest these absolute forces of God. God single-handedly created these unique and individualized energies. A multitude of blueprints arose out of the mind of God and He channeled these energies into forms of nature.

Through channeling, we can learn to appreciate the intricate beauty, the recurrent and interlocking patterns, and the unbelievably intelligent interlocking life forms. We pay tribute to the work of God as divine mathematician, divine musician, and a divine architect. Even the greatest scientists, who claim to be atheists, must admit that the design of the total universe is comparable to a masterful intelligence.

We have been able to improve upon nature, but only in small increments. Nothing can, or will, ever compare to the masterful work of God. Any attempts at improvement have consistently proved to create unanticipated side effects over time.

The original designs of the universe bore all the aspects of nature in one interlocking masterstroke of work. Many people call this superior design (or creative intelligence) the Creator – God.

Fundamental Lesson

We take creation as the fundamental lesson. Spirit is the life, the mind is the builder, and the physical is the result. This is a major step in the formula for creation, and it is the basic process for channeling and surrendering. This is the analogy given to us throughout this book, and within the realities of life.

One of the most important philosophical insights comes from what is known as the 'theory of emptiness.' To elaborate; at the heart of the matter there is this deep recognition – a fundamental disparity between the ways in which we perceive the world, including our own existence in the world, and the way that things actually *are* in the world.

In our day-to-day experiences we tend to relate to the world and to ourselves, as if these entities possess self-enclosed, definable, discrete, and enduring reality. If we examine our own conception of reality, we will find that circumstances are not as self-enclosed or definable as previously thought.

If we examine our inner self, we find that we tend to believe in the finite core of our being, rather than a continuum from the self to the divine. It is this war that characterizes our individuality (and identity) as an ego, in control. This can lead to an independence of physical and mental elements that constitute our human makeup – existence. This philosophy, or theory of emptiness, reveals that this is not only a fundamental error, but also the basis for attachment, clinging, and the development of our numerous judgments and prejudices.

A Channel of the Subconscious Mind

I am going to introduce a couple of ten-dollar words: 'disassociation,' and 'automatism.' Disassociation is the treatment of someone, or something as distinct and unconnected. Or, conversely, being treated in such a way. Automatism is an involuntary, organic function, physical reflex, or involuntary activity of the body. These are terms from the psychology of the subconscious mind and altered states of consciousness. Like ignoring the voice of intuition, this is another example of not following through with a first thought and making a wrong turn or judgment.

We usually think of the subconscious mind as simply a storehouse of memories. And filling it, not much different than filling a container. In reality the subconscious is a subsystem of the mind. It has intelligence. It perceives and it thinks. The subconscious mind manages the working of the body and the habitual aspects of our lives. This is a very important job.

If the conscious mind had to run everything we would have to move very slowly. We would have to think about every step that we take, every action, every word, every breath, and every heartbeat. This would drive us crazy. Fortunately for us, our brains naturally delegate these responsibilities to the subconscious mind. It functions as our caretaker.

For example, our conscious mind wakes up in the morning and we say, "I must get out of bed and get dressed." While we busy ourselves thinking about the day, the subconscious mind takes over and follows our instructions. It lifts our legs out of bed. It takes us into the bathroom and brushes our teeth. We do not pay much attention to these actions. All details of our actions occur as automatism reflex action directed by the subconscious.

FIGURE 12

Perspective

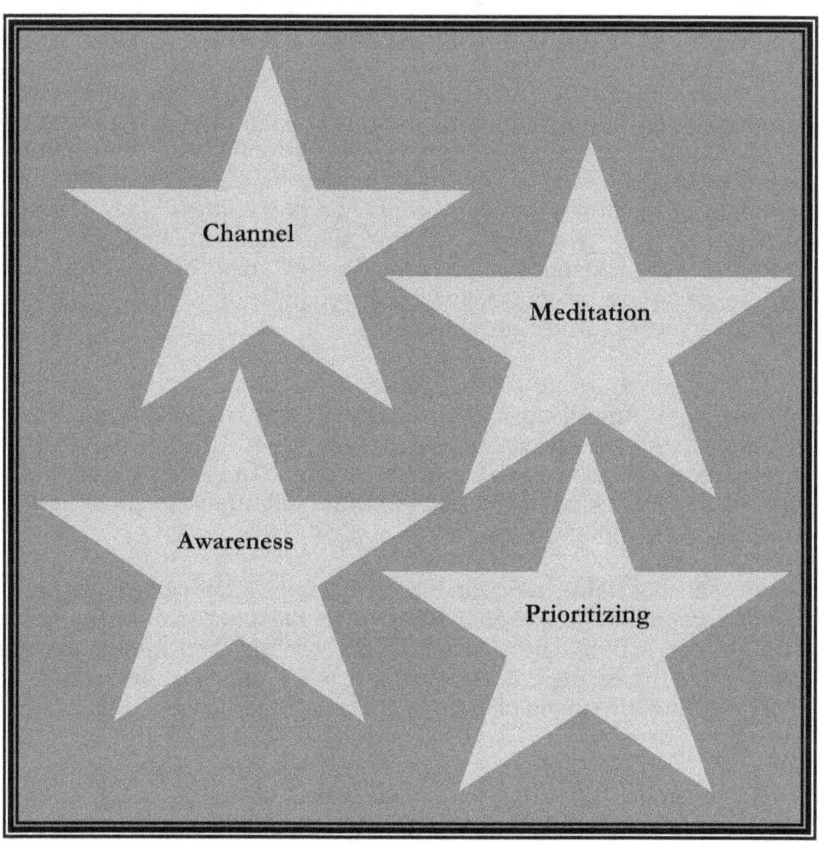

A Channel of Awareness

Sometimes we get so upset that we can hardly think straight. If a crisis catches us by surprise, our minds rule with thought or worry. Hundreds of different possibilities run through our mind. Things we might do and things that might happen appear all at once. It is hard to control ourselves and make plans. We need to get a hold of ourselves and gather our thoughts. We need to relax and clear our heads so that in a few minutes it is easier to gain perspective on the situation.

As we quiet down our thoughts, it becomes easier to clear the head and see things in a new light. This is the beginning of prioritizing values or needs. I'm sure you have had the same experience. You recognize that when you calm down you gain perspective, without pressure, and think more clearly.

With this first-hand knowledge of what it feels like to gain your composure during a traumatic event (or what *feels* like a traumatic event), you can now determine a simple set of factors to develop a solution to an overwhelming situation.

Achieve Calm

You will learn to extend that calm further with a clearer perspective. Achieve an absolute calm, and we might expect to achieve an absolute perspective. "On a clear day we can see forever." Or, as a Zen teacher would say: "When the water becomes still and quiet, you can see clear to the bottom."

In life, we must become quiet to hear our real heart. It is 'coherence' (uniform wave pattern) that gives a laser beam its power. Uniformity of thought between head and heart produces a moment of laser-like coherence.

As we calm ourselves in meditation, and quiet our thoughts, we too become more coherent and tap into a more powerful intelligence. It is like rising above the fray to become a silent eagle floating high in the sky. We then access a greater awareness and a larger perspective with all the wisdom that we might wish for.

FIGURE 13

Concepts within Self Awareness

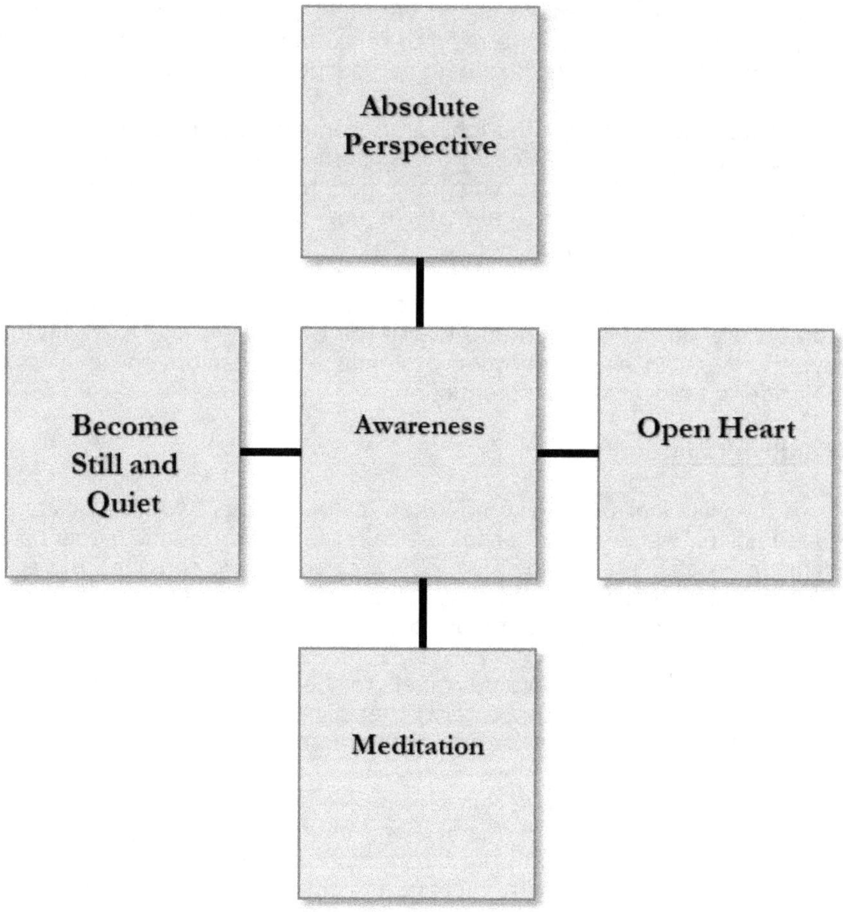

Challenge of Identity

The very nature of a man is determined by his reaction to conditions. His true identity is moral only if he affirms it to be. All conditions are an invitation to insight, to growth, to identity, and to re-affiliation. Looking at one's self, one needs to pay close attention to the awareness of honesty, at its deepest meaning. We must face the reality of who we are without moralizing. Only by knowing who we are, with clear insight, can we know what we must change in order to become what God meant us to be.

CHAPTER 6: ANXIETY

Anxiety

Everyone is spending at least fifty percent of his, or her, psychic energy keeping repressed memories below the level of consciousness. We can also say that each of us spends a great deal of our psychic energy trying to avoid anxiety. If this energy can be made available for creative living, we can change our lives, and destinies, and surrender to win. Behind every activity, every decision, every long or short-range plan, there is a conscious effort to avoid anxiety.

Since anxiety is painful to experience, we go to elaborate lengths to avoid situations which will produce it. We plan, rationalize and even lie to ourselves and others to avoid anxiety.

Avoid Anxiety

Psychologists agree, in general, that every action is an effort to avoid anxiety. A family in lack creates anxiety. So, a man goes to work, although he dislikes his job. His dislike becomes contempt, and this contempt causes or creates more anxiety.

At any given moment we are doing the thing that we prefer to do. The way we rationalize our conduct, to avoid anxiety, is illustrated by a man who dislikes social events. The man has been shy and withdrawn since childhood. He is without close friends to which he can relate. He recalls a sense of being alienated from his father and older brother. Now, in his 50s, he experiences an intense dislike for all social events, feeling in no way peaceful. The ease and peace one *should* experience while attending church eludes this man and he feels uneasy.

It is said by many professionals that all anxiety stems *not* from rationally thought out processes, but from emotional factors. And the roots usually go far back into childhood.

Pattern of Change

Trying to change our pattern of behavior without understanding our basic nature tends to create additional anxiety. And we tend to cling to a familiar course of action.

The course of action taken by some person may impress us as foolhardy, reckless, unwise, or just plain irrational. But to the person involved, being who (and what) he is, it appears to be the best possible choice. He is acting on certain emotional needs, assumptions and responses. And for him to act in any other manner would create in him marked tension and anxiety.

Hostility and Anxiety

Much anxiety is produced by repressed hostility. There are several ways of handling hostility or any other negative emotion. One may express it, suppress it, repress it, or release it to God in complete abandonment. There are situations where hostility may be expressed to the benefit of all concerned. At other times, to express deep resentment would be unwise and destructive. In such cases we learned to suppress the feeling. We know the feeling is there, and we are aware of it, but we suppress it.

The most dangerous option, which is largely used unconsciously, is to repress it. We pretend, to ourselves, that we do not feel hostility. For instance, a small child may feel hostility toward his parents. But he learns to bury or repress the feeling. Of course, we should not hate our parents. So, as In all other things that we do, we often learn to bury our feelings deep in the unconscious mind.

Inner Harmony

Through inner peace and harmony, the absence of self-destructive anxiety provides an emotional climate in which our bodies can function best. And our lives develop creatively. This is confirmed by the findings of modern science. However, it may not always pinpoint the cause of anxiety. And it may be true that there is nothing to worry about. Yet we may still experience a sense of defused anxiety.

This anxiety, in its infancy, may be the result of having had (as a child) an authoritarian parent, or having had unrealistic standards set, or from feelings of rejection. Pervasive anxiety in an adult often stems from events which happened early in childhood, that have long since been buried deep in the unconscious.

FIGURE 14

Patterns of Change

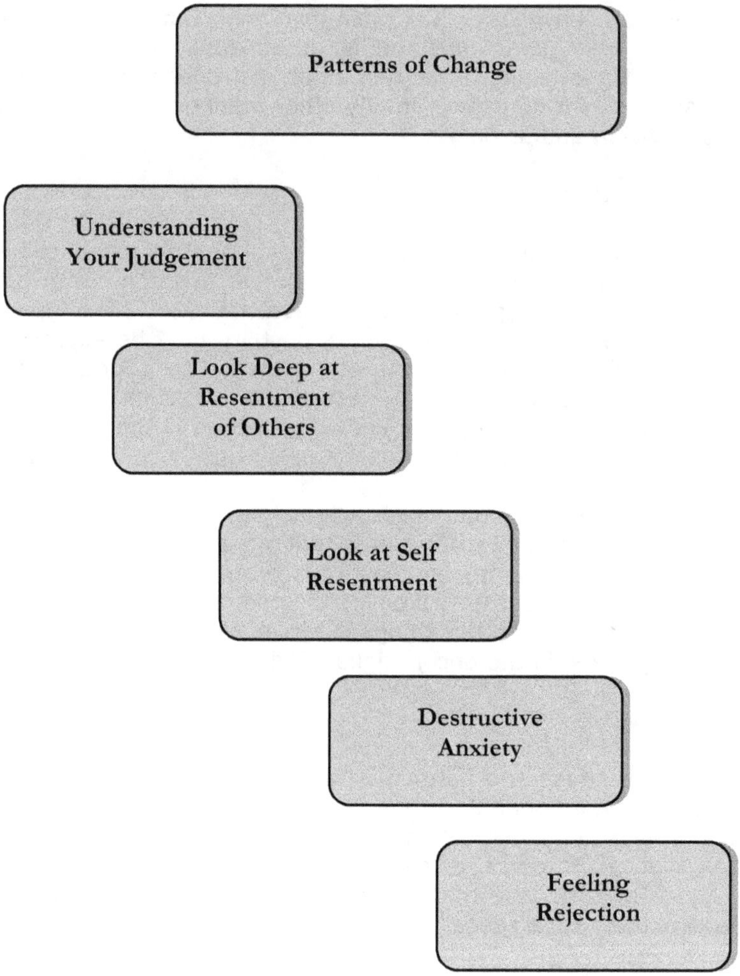

Patterns of Change

Understanding
Your Judgement

Look Deep at
Resentment
of Others

Look at Self
Resentment

Destructive
Anxiety

Feeling
Rejection

Suffering from Anxiety

Many people suffering from a high level of anxiety would rather have an operation, be hospitalized, or undergo painful treatment rather than facing the real fact that the problem is emotional or spiritual in nature.

Unconsciously, without any awareness of the mechanism involved, they choose to endure physical pain rather than acknowledge the emotional conflict outside and inside of themselves. Many doctors generalize that the vast majority of patients who complain of back and digestive symptoms have no organic disease which will account for their symptoms. Most prefer an operation or expensive treatment subsequent to receiving the news that their illness originates in their emotions. Not that these illnesses are entirely in the mind, or imaginary.

On the contrary, there is usually genuine pain involved, or at least mild discomfort. The pain is there, but all too often it originated in anxiety. Which is simply another way of saying that the problem is basically a spiritual one.

Whether we call it a mental problem, a spiritual problem or an impaired adjustment – we are talking about the same thing. Man is body, mind and spirit. And whatever affects one affects all. If there are inner conflicts, tensions, guilt or anxiety – at some point in his life the individual will tend to manifest this spiritual 'dis-ease' by some physical symptom. If he does not acknowledge the spiritual issue, his disease may manifest physical symptoms, or some form of mental illness. This is an unconscious need to punish one's self. He may become trouble prone, disease prone, bad judgment prone, or just plain bad luck prone.

Men have been known to make a succession of incredibly bad decisions, resulting in inevitable failure, when all their friends and relatives are united in warning against such decisions. This is a totally unconscious mechanism by which the *self* is punishing *self*, for real or imaginary guilt.

Handling Guilt

Guilt, whether real or false, can be handled in only two ways. It must either be forgiven or punished. If we cannot secure forgiveness, we find a way to punish ourselves physically, mentally or circumstantially. This seems to be an inexorable cosmic law.

It is not God who is punishing us, but rather the 'condemnatory self.' We *are* what we *think*. Guilt must be addressed. My book, "The Method of Forgiveness" takes a hard look at methods you can use to approach the area of forgiveness.

A Method of Cure for Anxiety

I believe that there are four main ways of escaping anxiety: 1) deny it, 2) avoid the thoughts, or feelings which arouse it, 3) rationalize it, 4) narcotize it. There may be only one creative way of handling anxiety on a permanent basis. The *real* problem is that we had feelings of guilt and self-criticism.

The only creative solution is to seek out and remove the source of anxiety. We must seek out the *source*. This is easier to suggest than it is to accomplish. Often, the roots are buried deep within the unconscious mind. One may be totally unaware, at the conscious level, of events which have created an undue amount of anxiety. Often, it is possible to seek out and deal with the source of the abnormal anxiety.

Feelings of shame, fear, inferiority and rejection are all at the roots and core of our anxious feelings. Time does not diminish our feeling of guilt. The passage of time may dim one's memory of this guilt, but the unconscious wants us to hurt from this guilt, creating a burden of needless anxiety. We need to know that fear brings a degree of upsetting anxiety.

FIGURE 15

Our Capacity to Deal with Anxiety

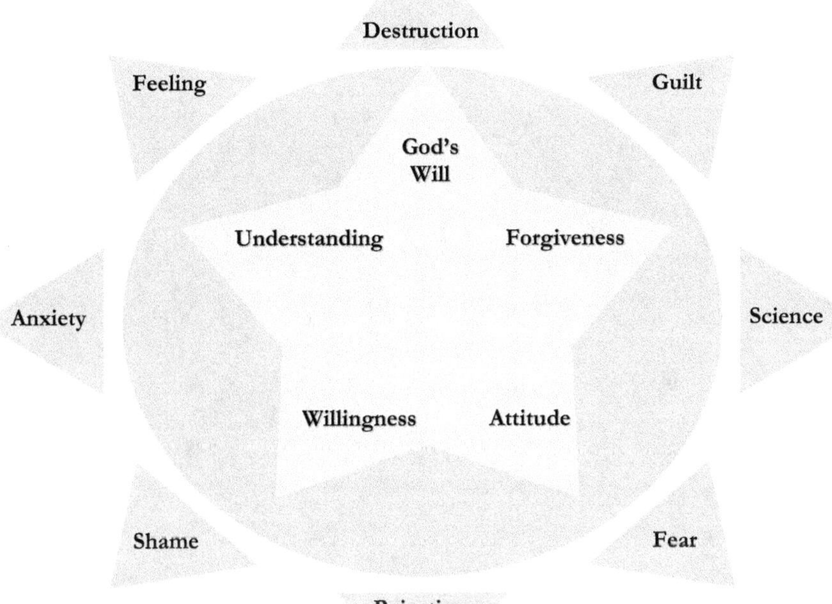

Divine Law

Whether we call it sin, guilt, anxiety, neurosis, or an illusion of the mortal mind, we are talking about the same thing. We are describing one who is out of harmony with divine laws, and thus alienated from God, his neighbor, and himself.

CHAPTER 7: GUIDANCE

Evaluating the Guidance

Do not get lost trying to pinpoint the exact source of, or channel to guidance. Try to detach from your human limitations. Focus instead on determining what part of the guidance is valuable. Evaluating the source is less important than evaluating the guidance itself. In fact, it is not possible to determine, with certainty, the exact source of channeled guidance. But rest in the fact that trying to find the answer is the best start.

Steps to Guidance

Take a common-sense approach to the matter of evaluating guidance. Ask yourself, does the guidance make sense? Does it speak to the present situation? Is it workable? Does it seem to be a constructive approach? Do you have a positive response to it? It is difficult to imagine how often these questions come up and been overlooked.

Examine the guidance from the point of view of the ideal that you set. If it does not meet the standard of your ideal, you should forget it. You may find that you have some soul-searching to do.

Assuming the guidance passes these preliminary tests, it is then time to obtain a second viewpoint or opinion. We should never put all our eggs in one basket. I strongly advocate that you never rely on a single external channel as a sole source of information. It is a good idea to compare it to other sources. For example: science, math, religion, spiritual meditation, prayer, and psychic materials are of great use.

Applying the Guidance

"Practice makes perfect." And "learn by doing." These phrases of garnered wisdom each express something of what is meant by "in the application comes the awareness." Hit or miss, we keep trying over and over again. Test guidance by applying it in practice. Determine if the guidance works. Try it out, test it and see for yourself – good old common sense.

By applying a piece of guidance, we not only test *it*, but we also test our *understanding* of it. Life acts upon us through our experiences and creates a greater awareness. And we are sure to learn from the experiences of the people who participate in our lives. We gain from each personal contact, more insight from the experience. Each contact and each experience build a clearer awareness of guidance. There are people that are full of insight, about themselves, but never seem to practice what they preach. They end up always spouting out the same idea, but they never change.

Grounding your Guidance

The practice of application is also grounding. Insights from the unconscious are full of energy. If ideas and symbols were simply contemplated, a person could become filled with energy to the point of danger. Control your focus on the matter, and the motivation, and do not give up.

FIGURE 16

Grounding Your Guidance

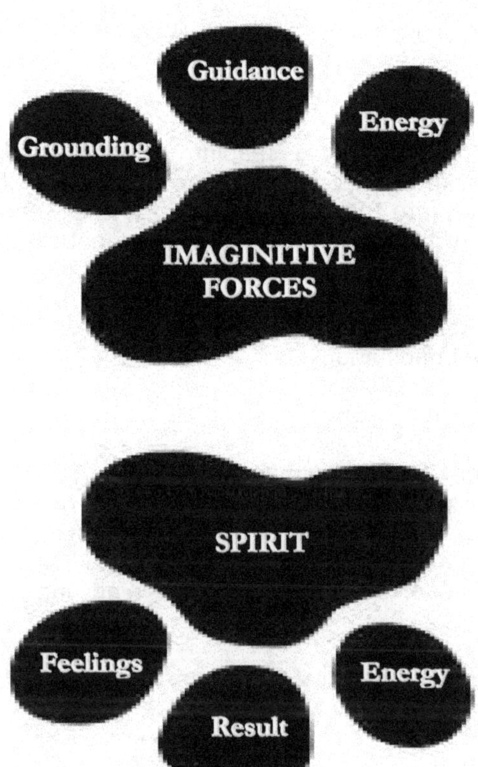

Imaginative Forces

"There is nothing as powerful as an idea whose time has come" – "thoughts are said to be things" – "imagination is reality." These statements turn our world inside out. They suggest that the world of the human mind is more real than the world of physical objects. Spiritual traditions share this point of view. The physical world is but a fleeting shadow. An effect and end-product of the mind's patterned projection of spiritual energy. Your spirit is your life. The mind is the builder of the blueprint – the physical is the result.

Shaping Energy

Our mental images exert a shaping influence upon energy, as energy precipitates into physical form. The process by which a pattern precipitates an idea into the conscious mind is the same process that transforms an idea into the manifest forms of nature. This influence can be called the imaginative force. The reason that imagination can *see* these invisible forces is because imagination is the generator of these patterning forces. The perceiver and the perceived have the same source – the imagination.

Connection with Imagination

The connection between imaginative *seeing*, and imaginative *creating* also exists within the endocrine system of the body. These glands govern the transformative bridges between mind and matter. They transform natural energy and spiritual energy into physical events. We experience this bridge between mind and matter through our feelings.

Feelings, while being physical sensations, are sensitive to the spirit. I believe that images in the imagination arise from our feelings. There is a connection between the activity of the pineal gland and the Leyden gland. This hormonal connection links "third eye" vision to the reproductive creativity of manifestation.

Times of heightened visionary imagination correspond to times of intensified creative feelings. This explains why the spiritual, mental and physical realms relate to the superconscious, subconscious, and conscious levels of the mind.

Wide Open Mind and Eyes

If the imagination sees the intrinsic forces, which forces do the eyes see? The imagination is not an alternative to seeing physical reality with the eyes. It is the psychic reality seen by way of the *wide-open* eyes. The imagination is the psychic (or intuitive) foundation, and formative background, for the physical eye's ability to see. In other words, we do our seeing through the *mind's eye*, not the eyeballs.

We cannot see what we cannot first imagine. Imagination is more basic than sight. What our eyes see merely adds physical details to what our imagination has already grasped through intuitive judgment.

Understanding Imagination

I know it is hard to understand. But by the time you finish this book you may better appreciate this puzzling relationship between imagination, perception, and the creative power of the mind. It is this equation, between mind and reality, that explains why there is so much overlap between someone channeling an energy and someone pretending to do so. Acting as if something were true has the effect of making it true.

Inspired Imagination

Sometimes, when we give the imagination free reign, it proves to be inspired or psychic. You may feel like you're just making it up or creating it yourself. You may later discover that your imagination was being receptive to patterns outside of your personal storehouse of knowledge. You can also have creativity of the imagination and shape your psychic influences. Whether we view it as inspired or psychic; both lure the imagination and channel patterns originating outside the boundaries of our own experience. I will point out that creativity, psychic influence, and inspiration have the same source – the soul.

Sometimes the superconscious mind exerts an inspirational or psychic influence on the imagination. It happened for me when I used to dream of controlling my thoughts. My imagination proved to be a channel for patterns in the thoughts of the universal mind. Through a process of pretending and role-playing, in a meditative frame of mind, my imagination channeled something from beyond my conscious knowledge.

FIGURE 17

Universal Mind

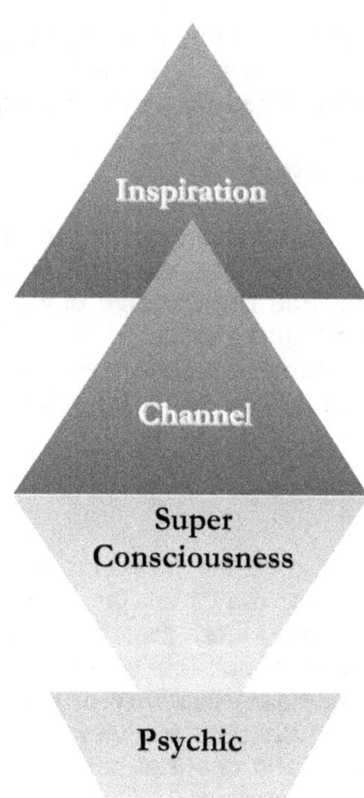

Ideas and Questions

Sometimes we don't know what we don't know. There is no question at first, just a problem. Just the sense of uneasiness, difficulty or pain. By yourself, or with the listening ear of a good friend, it is possible to analyze feelings of frustration or conflict, to determine what is needed by way of guidance. Perhaps the process could begin with the simple statement of the facts. "I am very dissatisfied with 'such and such,' and I want to know what to do about it." It helps to be more specific. What exactly is bothering you – and why? What are you seeking in a solution? What are your goals? What are your constraints?

Imagine this classic predicament. Behind door one is a fair maiden, representing good. Behind another door is a raging beast, representing evil. Let us make the predicament hypothetical. When the door of your choice is opened, the object behind the door will remain behind glass, for your viewing pleasure only. Now, let us make the predicament realistic. When the door is opened, the object behind the door will rush out to greet you or eat you. In which situation do you think that your powers of psychic guidance will be aroused to perform at their best?

The decision to ask for guidance, often comes only at the time the guidance is being sought. This intriguing enigma brings us back, full circle, to the beginning of our guidance heuristic. You should not ask the question if you are not ready to take responsibility for the answer. Knowledge unapplied is far costlier than the bliss of ignorance.

Healing the Channeling

Channeling the ideas of the higher self involves learning to channel the creative force itself. If you can teach yourself to develop a conscious relationship with this force, creation itself will be within your grasp. You can become a channel of knowledge and healing.

CHAPTER 8: AWARENESS

Awareness of the Unseen Forces

Perhaps you have been on the verge of becoming aware of these unseen forces. The invisible forces – the intelligence of creativity at work in all life – these are the *creative forces*. Spending time with nature teaches us how to meditate. Nature teaches about the hidden world of plants, animals and insects.

At the same time, humans being one with nature, contain these forces within us as well. They meet us within ourselves. And we can cooperate with their activity beyond ourselves, in the external world. Rather than seeking the creative forces with instruments directed outside of us, the secret is to look within. Focus on the *contact point* in our state of consciousness. In most cases we have been pushed or jolted into a position of pain or guilt before, quite by surprise, encountering the consciousness of these elements. It was by working hard to clear my mind that I came to believe in the forces of nature.

Confidence and Support

Girded with confidence in that external source of support, I reflected long and hard upon my experience. I realized that it was through my state of consciousness that I made contact. I also realized that the contact was made from within. It was not by squinting my eyes in some special way, or by closely scrutinizing world affairs, or through any external directive or maneuver.

Awakening the Power of Healing Forces from Within

We understand that the creative forces at work in nature also flow through our bodies. This energy is available for healing and regeneration. We can learn to awaken this force and become channels of healing. There is consciousness all throughout our bodies. Psychologists have demonstrated that with a little knowledge or training, subjects can make contact with individual cells within the body and affect their functioning. And that consciousness within the body exists at an even finer level than individual cells. Every atom reacts to consciousness.

Focus and Awareness

When we meditate, the ideal we focus on shapes our awareness. This altering of our consciousness filters down to every cell in the body and to every atom. It is important to set Christ consciousness as the ideal.

The closer we can attune ourselves to the idea of conscious oneness with God, the greater affects this ideal has upon the body. The consciousness of every atom within the body becomes filled with the awareness of God. God consciousness is in tune with creation, and thus able to be a channel for the force of creation.

Effect of Awareness

The effect of awareness alters the very rotational power forces themselves within the heart of every atom. Modern physics has learned that atoms are in constant and instantaneous communication with one another. Specifically, what it seems to communicate is the information contained in the rotational activity within the atom. It is something about the spin of energy within the core of the atom that serves as an instantaneous telepathic link between all atoms. I think that linking the effect of the rotational forces within the atoms of the body, during deep meditation, opens a channel for the healing force of creation on a more profound level.

FIGURE 18

Spirit

Imagine for a moment, allowing the conscious mind to become absorbed in the awareness of *oneness* with all life; good and bad. And then use God for the judgment. You, all the way from your conscious awareness, down to the very atoms of your body are resonating in harmony with the basic creative energy of life itself.

Life Force

Having awakened this connection with the life force, we can direct it. We can direct it with our hands through touch. We can also direct it with our minds by sending our prayers of healing to others. We all, at will, can send telepathic influence to the subconscious mind of other individual. They, through their subconscious mind, will pick up the pattern in our prayers and the atoms in that person's body will respond accordingly.

This has been proven, again and again, through personal experiences. The atomic structure of the receiver's body will align itself to the sender's subconscious emanations. We should strive to transmit balance and harmony. We can transfer the healing power expressed in our own meditative atonement.

It is awesome to realize that we can meditate on our oneness with God, to awaken the atomic power of the life force that is alive within us. It is even more awesome to contemplate our ability to become channels of this power; focusing it outside of ourselves to affect the atomic forces within another living being. As awesome as it may be to contemplate, research suggests that it is true.

Learning to be a Channel

Learning to be a channel of healing requires us to learn to act in a positive and constructive attitude of gratitude. We must repeatedly focus on the value of little things that count.

Ever notice the value of the smile? It is one of those little things that can make all the difference. Lending a hand, reaching out to touch someone, giving a hug – all of these little acts are as valuable as the laying on of hands – as valuable as a prayer.

Open your ears and heart without judgment. Take time to listen rather than give advice. A listening ear can be more effective in helping a person than all the suggestions we might conceivably offer.

Attitude of Understanding

To become a channel of healing, it is important for us to understand that it is not our job to fix or reassure people. It is important that we do not judge one another and that we keep our thoughts positive. Our thoughts are not private. They affect those around us. Thinking kindly of others is as important as acting in kindness.

Positive Attitude

Maintaining a positive attitude is important to our own personal health as well as in becoming a channel of healing. A good attitude helps your emotions and health. A positive attitude and good emotions help the endocrine system. Today we have a better perspective on life. Modern holistic medicine now recognizes, through countless research studies, that a positive attitude has a definite positive affect on the body's immune system. This, in turn, naturally makes us feel better.

In learning to be a channel of healing, all the other principles that we have learned in other aspects of channeling apply. In particular, attune to an ideal and set yourself aside, allowing the will to express itself. This applies, especially, in being a channel of healing.

Self-Doubt

Nothing is achieved through self-doubt. Be a channel for blessings. Above all, do not stand in your own way. The final secret of learning to be a channel is the hardest of all. It is also the simplest. It is that being yourself – your real and true spontaneous, essential, genuinely individual self – is the best way to be a channel of blessing to another.

CHAPTER 9: SURRENDERING

Being Yourself – Surrendering

Nothing is impossible for God. The time to act is now. Whoever, wherever, whatever – now is the time to start your path toward the *able to*. Let go of all that holds you back from ultimate surrender. For the influence of such a hard thing to do, all men seek this underlying power of all powers. There is a great cry in the earth today, and today is the acceptable time. You are spirit in a physical channel. You will experience that spirit by becoming aware of your *accepting* attitude, and ability. If we use this power as a crutch to simply compensate for a low self-image, rather than allowing it to touch and heal the problem, we cheat ourselves of the value of learning to surrender.

As we have grown up from childhood, we have all suffered wounds causing us to doubt ourselves and our true value. Psychologists who have studied the development of surrender find that people use their wounds as a motivation develop an alter-ego that is confident, spontaneous and trustworthy. Learning to actively practice surrender brings blessings that heal our self-doubts and teach us that we are okay and worthwhile. Otherwise, learning to surrender can be a self-defeating, self-deceptive experience.

Surrendering is basically a creative process. The spirit is the life. The mind is the builder. The physical is the result. And this is the basis for surrender. The mind sets itself on an idea which determines the pattern through which the spirit flows. The formula for surrendering is this – set the idea, then set one's self aside to let the idealized spirit express itself. The result is an inspiration, and then an action that serves the idea.

Example:

1) Let go of your hurt feelings towards someone who has injured you.

2) Aspire to let God take away negative feelings and help you to become able and willing to do the right thing.

3) Allow your spirit to have blind faith. Totally let go of it – completely.

Surrendering involves getting out of the way so that an idea or feeling can express itself through you. Surrendering to intuition, for example, requires the setting aside of our rational mind to allow inner knowledge to materialize. Regardless of the surrender modality, learning to step aside to remove oneself as an impediment is part of the process.

Hard Parts of Surrender

It is not that easy to be conscious of self without being self-conscious. We constantly hedge our bets. We cover our light with all kinds of baskets. Our self-doubt gets in the way. We have insecurities. We are concerned about what the others might think. Our pride will not let us risk making a fool of ourselves. We wish to remain invulnerable to criticism. We cannot afford to lose control or surrender our protective mechanisms. It is hard to set self aside without resorting to doing away with the self.

Learning to surrender oneself involves learning self-acceptance when we meditate. Our typical thoughts and worries pour through our minds. Yet we continue to meditate. Returning to our focus we gradually become more relaxed in our surrendering drive. Thoughts and worries continue to pass by, but we are so relaxed and intent on letting go that we easily ignore them. They do not bother us anymore. They do not disturb the final covering of peace.

FIGURE 19

Conscientious Surrender

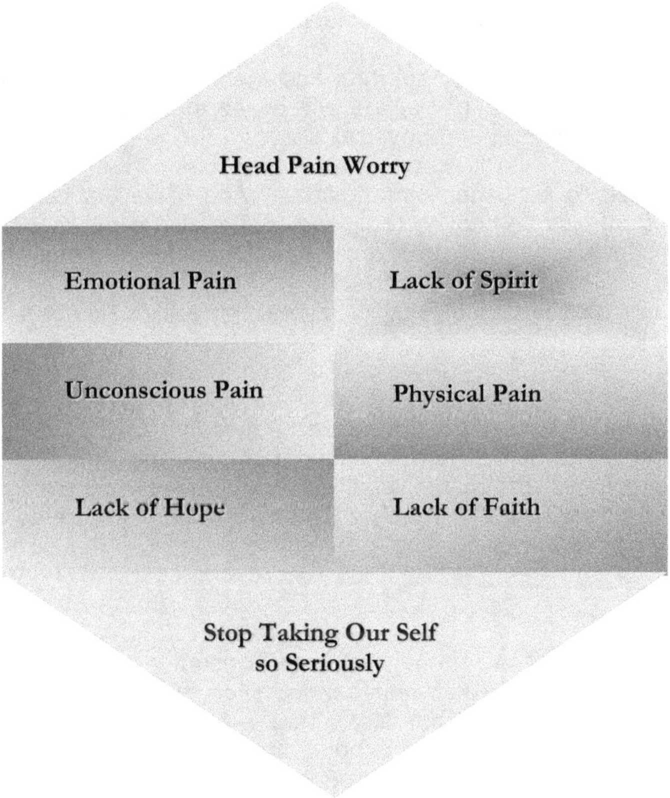

Faith, Healing, Prayer

These attributes are a certain way of thinking, a certain mental attitude and a certain way of believing. They are an uplifting process – a way of saying that I must believe in God. We are catapulted into a state of spiritual awareness.

Prayer

We come to understand that the answer to prayer comes from believing in the prayer. The action of prayer sets in motion the law of faith. And faith is the fundamental law of the universe.

Man's life is, in reality, spiritual and mental. And until his thought life is healed, no form of healing will be permanent. We understand that health is a mental *and* physical state.

"We seek to heal man's mentalities." And if we are successful in this, we shall also be healing their bodies. We also know that if we are able to see a new perfect man, he will appear. We feel that the spiritual, or *real* man, is perfect. And we seek to uncover this perfection which is within reach in every man's life. This is a spiritual mind healing.

Man can deliver himself from sickness, in the exact proportion to his discovery of himself, and his true relationship to the whole law of mind and spirit. The relationship of mind and spirit must be understood if we are to be used, by God, for definite purpose. The spirit knows, and the mind obeys. This is the inner nature of the *real* man. *This* is the law of his life.

Hope

The embrace of the thought of hope consumes some people. It is only through humility that hope enters. For the person who is just looking for hope, without humility, there is only chance. If the course of this life leads to God, there is hope after all. Within the limits of the human condition, what greater hope is there than the hope that allows one to escape from the condition of no hope at all?

Early Christianity

The very hope of early Christianity and the spreading of the good news inflamed the ancient world. But in that leap that characterizes all existential thought – in that insistence in surveying a divinity devoid of surface, how can one fail to see the mark of faith in the unseen? Faith is self-pride abdicating itself, to save itself. The moral value of faith cannot be diminished in the eye of the man who calls upon it cleanly and clear of pride.

Lucidity – Acting

Lucidity (clarity of the mind) is transparent in nature. It may seem easy. But it flies in the face of earthly reason, to the point of seeming to be a mental illness. We are looking for the clear mind. Our minds must be clear to comprehend divine or extrasensory instruction. Extrasensory inspiration comes to the mind of the lucid thinker.

Conquerors and Surrendering

Yes, man is his own, and *he* is his only end. If he aims to have spirituality in his life, he must clear his mind of all rebellion and anger. Conquerors sometimes talk of vanquishing and overcoming, but it is always ourselves that we must overcome. Every man has felt himself to be equal to a god, at some time in his life. True, or not? True, we wish to express this thought, but this comes from the fact that in the flesh, we have felt the amazing grandeur of the human mind.

The conquerors are merely those men who are conscious enough of their strength to live constantly in, and fully aware of their grandeur. It is a question of arithmetic. They are capable of no more than mankind at its best. Therefore, they never leave the human crucible and they plunge into the seething soul of rebellion.

Man, and His Silence

Man (and his values) should maintain silence when its best to keep quiet. Knowledge of your personal experience is a luxury in human relationships. Maintain awareness of the rules of the universe. Be true to yourself and keep a positive attitude in all your relationships.

Churches and Power

We are not ignorant of the fact that most churches are against us. An anxious heart eludes the eternal. And most churches (divine, or political) lay claim to the eternal. Happiness, courage, retribution, or justice are all secondary ends for them. This is a doctrine they bring, and one must subscribe to it. Their concern with the eternal is an ongoing journey. The truth that falls within the scope of this book can be touched with the hand. I cannot separate reality from the feeling of the eternal.

At the end of it all, despite every effort, there is death. People beautify only what they love. Death repels us and tries our patience. But the fear of death must also be conquered.

Compromising Eternal

Some, without compromising, have chosen the eternal and deemed the world an illusion. Others feel pity for themselves, in the physical world. Self-pity seems to be the compassion that is most acceptable. It is a feeling we hardly understand. One that seems to lack virility. But we call the lucid ones virile. And there is no strength that is apart from lucidity.

No Judgments

Let me point out that these images do not propose moral codes. They involve no judgement. They are only sketches. They merely represent a style of life. The lover, the actor, the adventurer who makes mistakes – can also be the chaste man, the civil servant or the president of the republic if he wishes. We are all consumed in this day-by-day play of reality.

I wish to make an example of the extreme. At this level, the absurd gives people a royal sense of power. It is true that princes are without kingdoms, but they have an advantage over others. They know that all realities are illusions – real illusions. They know that this illusion is their whole nobility and it is useless to speak to them about hidden misfortune or the ashes of disillusion. "Being deprived of hope is not despairing. The flames of earth are surely worth celestine perfumes of faith." Neither I, nor anyone else can judge them here. They are not striving to be better. They are attempting to be consistent.

If the term 'wise man' can be applied to the man who lives on what he has, without speculating on what he has not, then he is a wise man. One of them is a conqueror in the realm of the mind. A lover of intelligence knows this. But best of all, we must not hold onto to judgment until we become wiser.

Indifference

Everything begins with the lucid indifference. Science, having reached the end of its paradoxes, ceases to propound and stops to contemplate the ever-virgin landscape of phenomena. The heart learns this – that the emotions that delight us when we see the world's wonders do not come to us from its depth, but from its diversity. Explanation is useless. You only have self and the universe, inexhaustible in quantity.

Self, marks both the depth and the diversity of our experiences. Still, our experiences are but monotonous, though passionate, repetitions of the themes already orchestrated by the world. We view inexhaustible images on the pediment of temples, forms, colors, numbers, and grief. Our bodies offer no escape for the intellectual element that reflect these images throughout a person's thoughts. But for the first time, we make the mind get outside of the itself. Not for it to get lost but to see it clearly and to understand our rationalizations.

Self-Statement of Self

We do not hate ourselves because we are worthless, but because we are driven to seek self and ignore others. Self-torture is inevitable for one that tries to whip himself into a perfection that is impossible to achieve. Hurtful accusations against self, or disparaging thoughts frustrate us. We are actually torturing *ourselves*.

Confess or be Punished

There is within us an inner mechanism which tends to enforce its own elicit confession or be punished. Either we must secure a sense of forgiveness and cleansing, or we find a way to be punished, or to punish ourselves.

The soul will run into its judge. Man is so constituted that his guilt must be the fully forgiven, or he will find ways, via an inexorable inner mechanism to punish himself. God has so constituted us that guilt must be resolved. We are concerned now, not simply with some overt guilt-worthy act, but with all thoughts that register on the Inner self as guilt; such as shame, inferiority, feelings of rejection or worthlessness. Those hurtful actions and thoughts guide our desires and impulses to make us feel bad.

God has instituted the mind forgiveness, and if our concept of God's unconditional love is adequate, we can accept his pardon and forgive ourselves. However, if we cannot believe in the love that God has for us, we will not accept the long bridge that spans this gap in our lives. And we will not cross the bridge – for it is narrow.

We must continually remind ourselves that a person does not truly love until he loves himself – until he learns the process of forgiving the old self. We learn to love God's plan and acquire the capacity to love others, unconditionally, without harsh judgment.

Although the logic of past performance guaranteed another wrong choice, that wrong choice was never made. This shows us how illogical logic can be with harsh judgment. We thus take on the new attitude that we are right in acting in a manner counterintuitive to our past actions. The wrong choice was never made, not because we suddenly got smart, but because we made the decision that God cares for us.

God moved me to attend my first therapy group meeting. In that room, God opened my mind and heart to the meaning of something other than the knowledge of men. It was the power that helped me make a major change in my life. Years spent in these groups have helped me in my search for meaning. First, to *see* me (self-understanding). Second, to *free* me (self-acceptance). And, finally, to *be* myself – to love relentless honesty with my past guilt, and constantly increase my love, and decrease my harsh judgment of others. I grew into a new life of *meaningfulness*.

FIGURE 20

Forgiveness

Free

For myself, I am certain that to whatever degree I can *see* me, *free* me, and *be* me; I can now try harder to love God with all my heart, mind and soul.

Walk into Perfection

Life is an infinitely good and ultimately intelligent power. This is the law of the universe. To man, the inner sanctuary of all possibilities in life, there are no limits or bounds to reaching the power of understanding self.

Ignorance

In our ignorance, if the truth that we have misused cost us the highest power we possess – our freedom, then by absolute law that misuse of power has brought upon us that bounded condition in which we suffer. We are bound because we were first free. The power that appears to bind us is the only power in the universe which can set us free. As you believe – as you collect your view of faith in a higher power within the universe, you become free of the bondage of judgment. If not faithful, we suffer, as symbolized by heaven and hell. Not because suffering is imposed upon us, but because we are ignorant of our true nature. We are unaware of the spirit within self, because we have blocked our minds from freedom, with fear. Not ever understanding the why of it at all.

CHAPTER 10: SPIRIT AND SPIRITUALITY

Spirit of Power

Power of the spirit spreads itself over the whole universe and shoots at us from every angle. But it can only become power to us when we *recognize* it as power.

We cannot enter because of unbelief. We can only enter in because of our belief. Faith is a mental assertion elevated to the point of realization. It is beyond the mere quibbling or mumbling of words of prayer. Prayer identifies itself with reality in such a manner that reality becomes real to the believer. The invisible becomes visible to the lucid mind.

Avoiding the Spirit

Behind every activity, every thought, every decision, every long (or short) range plan there is an unconscious effort to avoid the spirit. Since we cannot truly understand the spirit we plan, rationalize, work, even lie to ourselves and others in an effort to avoid it. Psychologists agree, in general, that every action is an effort to avoid the responsibility to the spirit.

Becoming Spiritual

The first method is not to avoid the existence of the spirit. It requires a conscious process in having faith, *in* faith. The individual is conscious, all the while, that certain distressing or painful symptoms that block us off from the spirit could be emotional and physical.

The Law of Cause and Effect

When one gives a treatment for right action and does not believe that right action will be the result, he makes his own treatment negative. Therefore, we should spend as much time (and thought) as it takes to convince ourselves of the truth of our thoughts and actions. Now this is not a power of will, but a power of choice.

If one doubts his ability to make an effective choice, he should say something like this: "I am convinced that these words and thoughts have power. And I believe in it. I will trust in it to produce the right results in my life."

We should work, not with fear, but with expectancy. Not by coercion, but with conviction. Not through negative compulsion, but in a state of conscious recognition and receptivity. We do not have to deprive or push. But we must accept and believe. Then we can, and should, leave everything to the law, expecting a fully complete proof of our spirit and faith.

Method of Cause and Effect

We learn how, and when, to use the law of cause and effect. We do not put the power into words, but we do let power of the law flow through the words. Whoever most completely believes in the *power* will produce the best results.

Attitude:

This is a *mental* attitude toward an open mind – toward the principal of the living life. Spiritual things must be spiritually discerned. And when we are ready, and spiritually willing to discern, we shall find a ready response from the invisible into the visible. We make our best decision and leave the results to that law which is perfect. Hopefully, readers (those of us without ego and arrogance) will have gotten the idea here. It is totally out of our control. Perfection is not of us, it is of God, through which all things are possible – the one and only higher power.

> Our mind must be steady in its conviction that our life is some part of God, and that the spirit is incarnate within us (visualizing faith)

Faith

The universe is a spiritual system. A system of laws and intelligence. One approach is through the mind, and this point of entry enables us to know, will, and act upon our will – good or bad. Faith and belief are closely related mental attitudes and choices. Faith has been recognized as a power throughout the ages, whether it be faith in God, faith in ourselves or just old-fashioned stubbornness of will to make it happen. Faith is a faculty of the mind that finds its highest expression in the religious attitude. But even the man who has faith in his own ability accomplishes far more than one who has no confidence in himself. Those who have faith have great power.

The Great Truth of Reality

Why is it that one man's prayers are answered, while another's remains unanswered? It cannot be that God desires good for one person and not for another. It must be that all persons, in their prayers and approach to reality, receive results; not because of what they believe in, but because of their belief (and faith) is an affirmative mental approach to reality.

Understanding Faith

The thought of faith molds the undifferentiated substance and brings into manifestation the thing which was fashioned in the mind. When we dismiss fear, we can use our creative imagination and strong faith. There will never be any of the eternal values, like beauty and love, without faith. There will never be an end to God, nor any of the attributes which are co-eternal and co-existent with God.

Spiritual Substance

The fact is that all around us, waiting to be formed, is the divine urge or thought. It is God's way of letting us know that we should act upon the thought. Look at your judgment system and understand that most of our lives we made decisions based on self, and on feelings. Feelings are actions, and faith brings us back to a reality of understanding that we can only take a step forward toward God's will and plan.

God's Plan

We are all looking for the direct intuition from God. We must keep ourselves in a state of equilibrium, poise, peace and confidence. Look for a state of spiritual understanding. The science of faith will be one of the most important steps in this quest for enlightenment. Do not give up on yourself.

Principle of Faith

When we fail to realize that this principle is not bound by precedent, we limit our faith to that which has already been accomplished through intuition. Faith finds its proper place under divine law. There is no limitation. And miraculous results follow.

If we are to have an active faith – the faith *in* faith) – the faith of God instead of merely a faith *in* God, our thoughts must be centered in the universal mind. We are convinced that under divine law all things are possible.

Such faith comes from growth, knowledge, and life experience; hit or miss, as you keep trying. We must cling steadfastly to the knowledge that God is good, and that God is underneath all, and full circle around all thoughts, ideas, feelings, and hope. God will never leave you.

Power of Thought

It has taken man thousands of years to learn that he has the power to control his own destiny. "As a man thinking in his heart – so is he."

Shakespeare is accredited with the saying, "There is nothing, either good or bad, but thinking makes it so." It is one thing to know a principal, another to apply it.

Infinite Intelligence

This principal to understanding the process of thought is that we are surrounded by intelligence. It makes possible the act of healing physical disease, changing our environment, attracting friends, and demonstrating the power of right thinking. We are in the presence of an infinite mind which will back our thoughts according to law.

Being a spiritual being, we do sense the presence of an intelligence which is totally beyond human comprehension; an intelligence which is great enough to encompass the past, to better understand the present, and to be aware of the future.

Studying the Power of Thought

We are living in an intelligent universe, which reacts to our thinking process. To the extent that we learn to control the mental thinking states, we will automatically control our personal environment. This is why we are studying the power of thought as we approach the subject of spiritual mind power. This is how, and why, we look at our own thoughts.

In the great universal mind, we are the center of intelligence, and every time we think, we set the mind into action.

The Universal Mind

We do not create. We use the power of the One Power which created us. The sooner we realize this, the sooner we shall be able to work in line with the spirit.

Law of Life

The law of life is a law of thought. The spirit can do for us only what it can do *through* us. The power behind all things is without limit. But in working *for* us it must work *through* us. The power is limitless. We do not understand this fully because we are in self-doubt in most spiritual matters. We cannot, in most cases, turn our will completely over to this limitless power.

CHAPTER 11: THE SPIRIT AND HEAVEN

Steps to Heaven

Through spiritual discernment we can now see that we have within us a power which is greater than anything we shall ever own. A power that can and will overcome every obstacle in our experience and give us clarity, peace, healing, and a new life.

> If God is for us, who can be against us?

Immortality and Heaven

"And no man has ascended up to heaven but He that came down from heaven, even the Son which is in heaven."

Here is another of those hidden meanings, which places Jesus among the great mystics. He said that no man can go to heaven unless he came from heaven, and that he can neither go to, nor come from heaven unless he has already been there. We have tried to show you a way of living in the now based upon making yourself an open channel. If applied, honest healing and a better understanding of ourselves and others will result. We must work on the mind and body, but most importantly, the great and clear open channel to the spirit.

> Truth knows neither yesterday, today, nor tomorrow. It knows sequence but not time – only that we return to God's heaven. And since heaven is not a place, but a state of consciousness, the return must be a recognition that heaven is already within.

> The Son of Man, who is also the Son of God, was already in heaven, and on the earth at the same time.

Immortality means that we shall persist after the experience of the true physical death, retaining a full recognition of ourselves, and in most cases recognize others.

Anticipate Future Events

Individuality might remain without remembrance. Not so with our personal judgment. What we are is the result of what we have been; the result of what our subconscious has been programmed to be – good or bad.

Visualizing Faith

Acceptance and trust are at the base of immortality. Faith in this process enters into our thoughts. If you can believe, your faith will be stronger. The foundation for correct mental acceptance is perfect God, perfect man, and perfect being.

> Thoughts must be organized to fit the premise, and conclusions must be built on the blueprint of the spirit.

Our Body

Our body is a concrete manifestation, existing in time and space, through the physical universe. In the body, God wanted a shell of mass that can be used each day and manifested in the form of the mind of God.

In the creation, our body needed a beginning and an end. The manifestation of spirit neither begins, nor ends. If the spirit is to come into self-realization, the body plays only a part of the matter.

Soul Search

In looking for a body to house the divine being, when we pass from this plane; shall we become spirit, or shall we have tangible bodies? The form of the body is necessary for self-expression. Consciousness is the base of the soul. It is one law of consciousness that houses the form.

Law of Mind and Spirit

The physical body is not changed by the physical body. But we ask; from what substance would the soul create a new body? We can only question the theory of God's work and only imagine what it looks like to step into heaven.

FIGURE 21

Stepping into the Divine

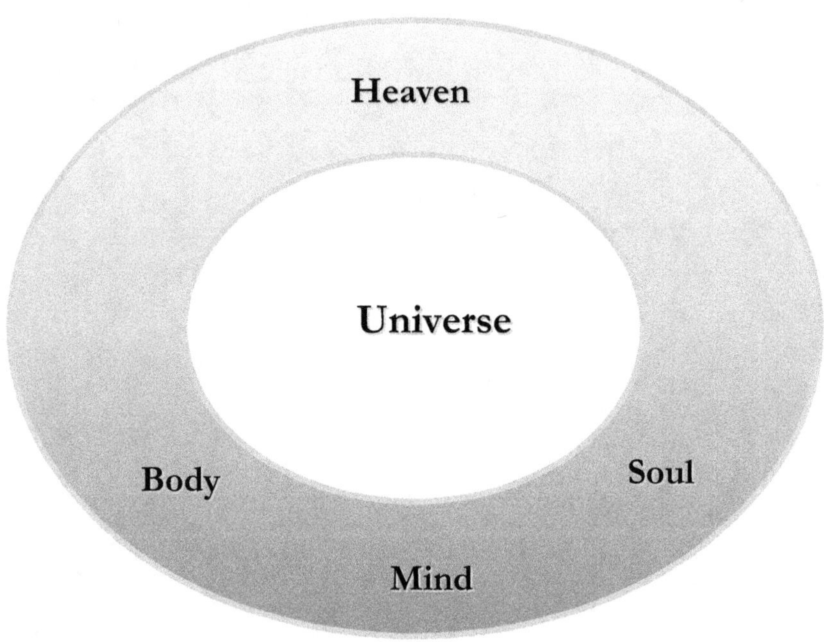

If instinct has molded the outer body into a definite form, why should it not mold the inner one into a definite form? There is every reason to suppose that it does, and no reason to suppose that it does not. Could it be that there is a body within the body, to infinity?

Life Control

There is, I believe, a continuum of a personal life. Our earthly lives and the afterlife stream in a continuum of consciousness, with a recollection of itself, and the ability to know, and to make itself known when the experience of physical death occurs. I *am*, and I will continue to *be*, beyond the grave. I wish to feel that I shall again meet those friends whose lives and influences have made my life happy while on earth. I will surely meet my family and friends on the other side. Yes, I believe one must understand that this is not the only life we will live.

Immortality

I believe that certain experiences have given us ample evidence to substantiate the claim of immortality. I do not base my belief in immortality on the revelation of anyone, but myself. I *believe* in other men's revelations. I am only *sure* of my own view of immortality – not a small dream, not a brief hope, but as a proven fact. Immortality is so completely demonstrated to be the way of things that it would not be far-fetched even to assume it the reason for death.

Spiral of Life

The spiral of life is upward and onward. Evolution carries us forward not backward. Expansion, eternal and progressive, is its law. And there are no breaks in the continuity. It seems to me that our evolution is the result of an unfolding consciousness of that which already is, and we need to realize it as a true fact.

Time and Healing

Time heals all wounds, adjust conditions, and time alone satisfies the expanding self and reconciles the visible with the invisible. We must give ourselves time to work out all the misunderstood problems.

We must work things out here or we shall work them out in the hereafter. There will be time enough in the eternity.

All men are an incarnation of soul eternity – infinity

Trust Life

> With all facts that we face, we should learn to trust life.
> The power within us wishes no ill will towards anyone.

> Life is good, and God is good. Just accept this and learn
> how to live in His grace.

No one needs to prepare to meet God. He meets us every day in our work, with our friends, family and loved ones. He meets us in the sun, in the joy of nature, and in His silence.

> So, it's heaven. And here's how we get there.

Note: we will make a big deal of this part of the book.

Dying

We prepare not to die, but to live. The manifestation of the thought of death should slip from our consciousness altogether. And when this action of great events of the heart and soul takes place, it should be a beautiful and glorious feeling. Experiencing this will, and does, go to our subconscious and our soul forever. The fact is that we only need to download this memory and act as though we are free of guilt and sin, because the choice is up to us. All things are possible with God's help.

FIGURE 22

Soul Progression

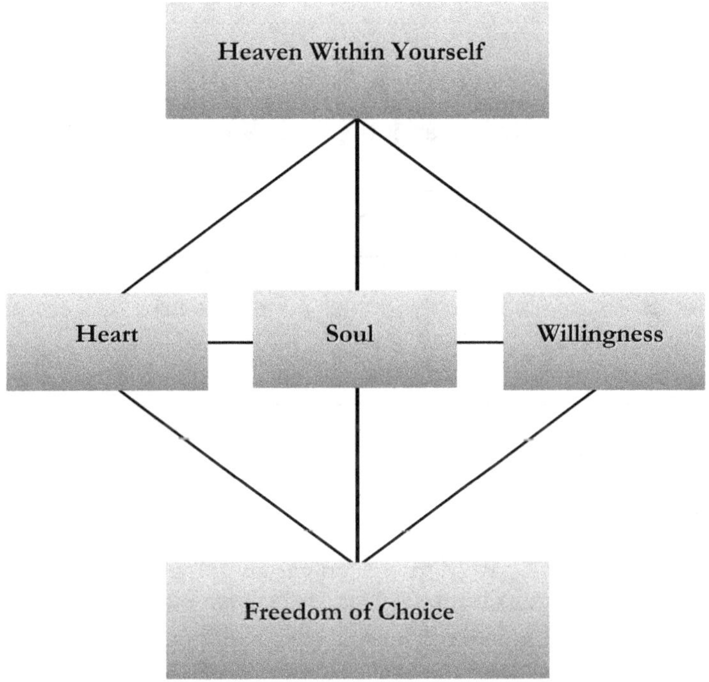

Subconscious vs. Soul

The conscious mind of mankind is self-assertive and self-knowing. It will choose to accept or reject. The conscious mind is the one and only part of man's mind which can think independently of all conditions.

> Statement of man. He does the right thing, wrong.

We face our God every minute of the day. There, the mind and soul are continuously unfolding into an open recognition of their real blueprint in the creative order of the infinite universe.

> The Spirit is Now

The spirit is really the only infinite mind on earth. It is eternal. It is complete, perfect, satisfied, and at peace with itself.

> Spirit-peace within Itself

Universal Unity

Spirit is God. God is spirit – a universal unity and wholeness. God is mind. The self-knowing mind of understanding. The conscious mind of man is part of the self, mind, soul-knowingness of the mind of God.

Angels glory

We can distinguish ourselves from other creation because of the divine self-knowingness. Man alone, can make a decision on his overall destiny – to determine what manner of life he shall lead. God created him but a little lower than angels and gave him the choice to glory and honor in the spirit.

We were all born of spirit, our soul is but a guidebook inspired by God's divine blueprint. Our souls are only an element in the great plan. Here is an invitation to breathe the vivid – to feel the fire in the heart's center and join the journey into the full flowing spirit of heaven on earth.

CHAPTER 12: UNDERSTANDING

Begin Where you Are

We feel that the elimination of our old way of judgment, and facing fear is but a beginning in the true search for spirituality. We are at the turning point. Every day we stand at the turning point. Our thoughts and actions can propel us towards growth and research in spirituality. Enlightenment stops the old way of life; full of bad habits and thoughts.

What must we do to change our selfish self-indulgence, and resistance to the flow of life? We must stop fighting our body, or anything else. We must find a way to surrender the old way and open our hearts to a power greater than our force on earth. We must find a way to understand the new way of living. That way is God, as our *now* turns to minutes.

Ernest Prayer

In prayer, as in life, we tend to place what we really want at the center of our souls. The neurotic tells us that he will do anything to be rid of his symptoms, but he will do anything rather than give them up. To him, they are preferable to facing and dealing with the real problem. And he gets what he wants most.

In prayer, we receive what is against our natural will. We may ask for what we want in prayer. But it is the soul's sincere desire uttered, or unexpressed that we will receive. If what we ask for in prayer verbally conflicts with the things we want, basically at the feeling level, we receive not what we asked for, but what is best for the evolving soul.

Indifferent Prayer

One might pray, "Oh Lord bless the poor in this country." But, if the prayer is rather indifferent about their welfare, then that is the nature and extent of the prayer.

One might pray to have some physical symptom removed. But, if in his heart he is unwilling to change the basic emotional attitude which has caused the symptom, he is simply saying, "I want the symptoms removed but not the root cause." But since the symptom cannot truly be dealt with apart from the cause, he gets precisely what he really prefers under the circumstances; which is to suffer with the symptom rather than to pursue a change of personality or attitude.

Prayer Verbalization

Prayer is not mere verbalizing. The words we utter have no real significance, unless they are a true reflection of what we feel or think. When what we say, and what we feel are in conflict, then what we feel is the real prayer.

Prayer is not merely words. Prayer is not an effort to change God or His intent for us. Prayer is an effort to bring our stubborn, reluctant, egocentric wills into harmony with His lovely, benevolent purpose. He wills the best for us. When we can trust His wise, creative purpose for our lives we will have begun to pray effectively.

Difficulty with Prayer

One difficulty is that most people who pray have little idea of what prayer really is. They assume that prayer consists of telling God about their problems here on earth and telling Him how to solve them. If little or nothing happens as a result, they assume that either they lacked faith, or that God has not answered their prayer. A good percentage of people believe in prayer, and even nonbelievers will give prayer a go in a crisis or bad spot of time. Still, the faith in prayer may be somewhat disparaged.

FIGURE 23

Beyond Self

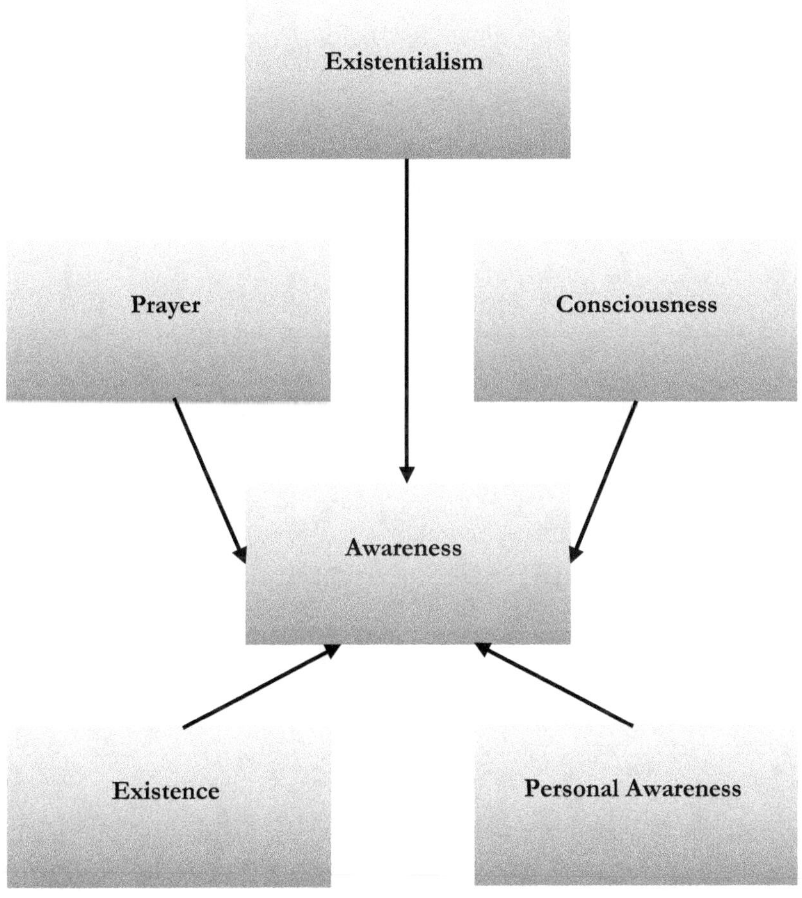

Human beings are personal beings who find themselves in an alternate reality universe. Whether or not God exists is a tough question; to be solved by reason of fact or thought, or both.

Faith does not start by merely believing in God. Existentialism, in theory, arrives at the same conclusion, but starts elsewhere. The theistic existentialism movement emphasizes the place in which human beings find themselves when they first come to self-awareness, or self-reflection for a moment. Try to be certain of your own existence, your own consciousness, and your own determinacy. This can be your starting point.

13: UNIVERSAL ACCEPTANCE

Ambivalence and Ambiguity

Is this human reality ambivalent? Do not the values of human love and compassion give evidence for a benevolent world? Let us consider hatred and violence. An impersonal universe points in the other direction. Perhaps we should love that which we cannot understand.

Absurdity Universe

Some say that God is immediately responsible for this absurd universe. Yes, we can believe in God, in spite of the universe. We can say that such faith is intellectual suicide. And some may agree with this statement. But while reason may lead to agreement, we can always refuse to accept reason's conclusions and take a leap toward faith.

Cosmic Consciousness

Perceive the wholeness of the cosmos. Learn how to become one with the whole of it with eyes wide open. Recognize that self is the generator of all reality. And in that sense both self and reality lie within the universal consciousness.

Ego Boundaries

Let go of the boundaries of your ego and experience the sudden identification with the thoughts of all life. Experience the thrill of electrical sensations and sense the expansion of your total judgment system. Then there will be no limits to your thoughts and boundaries.

The True Belief

Believe that you have awakened. And that the reality of the ordinary consciousness is but a poor, dark shadow. Now, we are free. Now. We have transcended time and space.

FIGURE 24

Meditational Consciousness

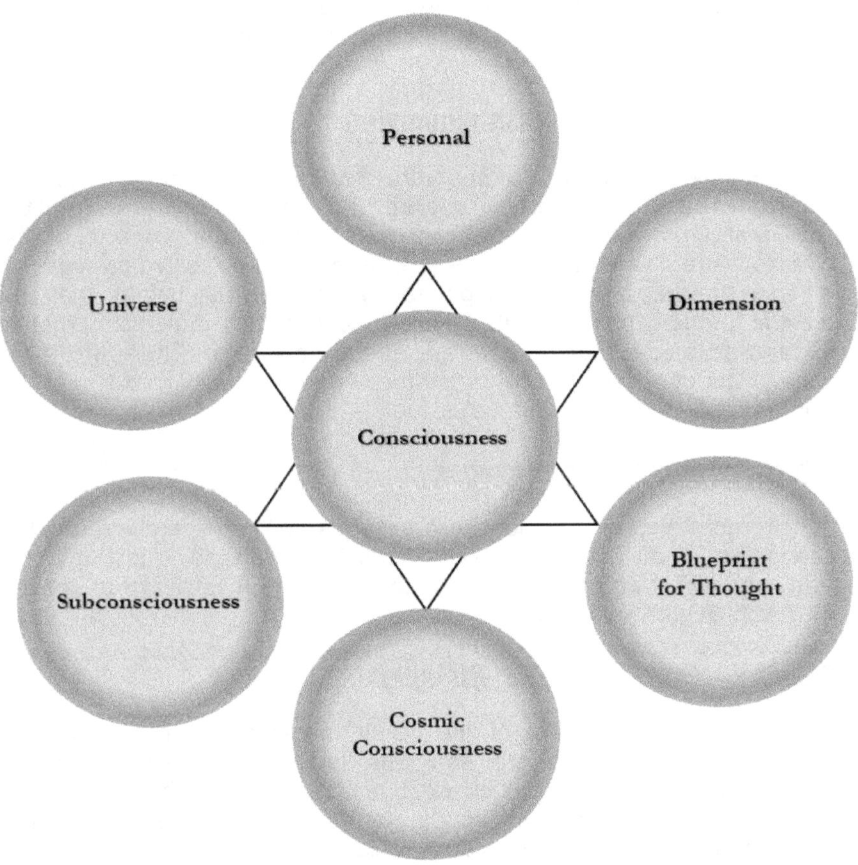

All Consciousness is not Euphoria

Not all people will understand you now that you are willing to forgive because forgiveness is contrary to the world's view.

State of Altered Consciousness

There are many details in this altered state of consciousness: timelessness, light, space, unlimited energy, and Magi beings. These are a private part of our universe. But they are open to the enlightened ones.

Universe Next Door – Fifth dimension

There is, we think, a separate reality. The total amount of information has not been blue printed. But where is this other reality? This reality is within our subconscious, self-cosmic consciousness. When we are aware of it, we can see, react to, and receive power from it. Then, perhaps, we can begin to control spiritual beings that are present outside of our limited access to the fifth dimension that is juxtaposed to the four that we are already aware of. There are three dimensions of space. The other is time. A fifth dimension exists, and it is important and true as the other four.

Altered States of Consciousness

Altered states of consciousness allow us to keep searching for that perception of this fifth dimension. Let's try to answer questions that lead the way of access into this dimension. One must learn to consult with self. Beginners beware!

Occult Version of the Fifth Dimension

This is the framework of the occult intellectual. Most, if not all, mediums, witches, sorcerers, shamans, witch doctors and others fall into this category. The ever-present crystal ball and the Tarot cards take us to the dark side. One should not go into this dimension without an introduction into the rites and systems of the occult. Step lightly into these areas of belief.

The Modern Version

Take this open door into the understanding of the mind and its multidimensional nature. The mind will always cross-examine our thoughts, feelings, facts, and fears. And the mind also works on spiritualism and ancient judgments of heaven and hell.

FIGURE 25

Symbol System

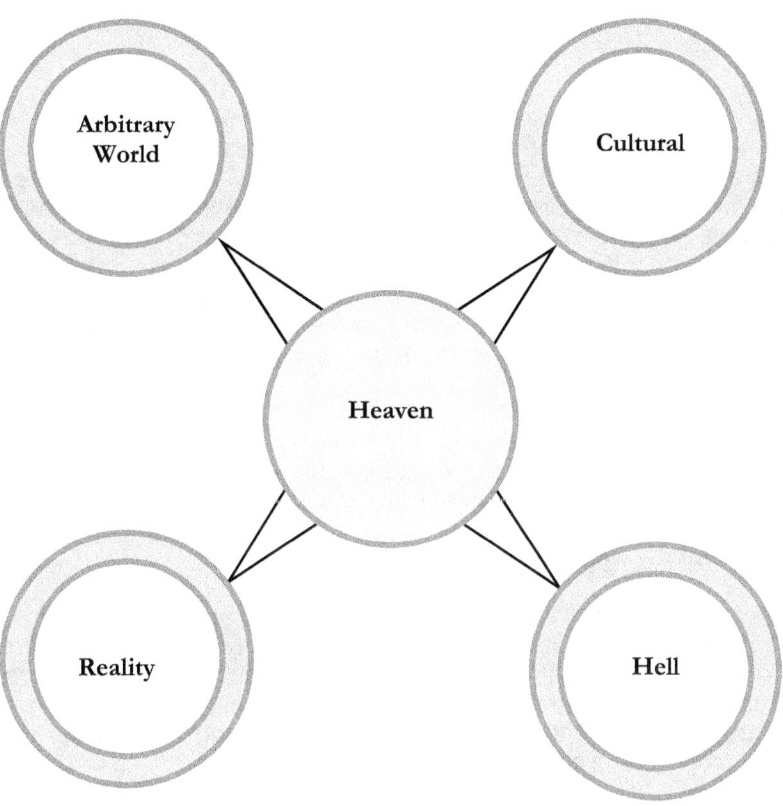

CHAPTER 14: INFLUENCE BY HEAVEN AND HELL

Heaven and Hell

Heaven and hell are not a part of our present reality. They are an arbitrary world of understanding in our value system, better looked at as a symbolic system. Such rules are made by man, along with a language system of cultural concepts of right and wrong. Western language, and its cultural concepts and influences manufacture this abstract environment. One must view each side (heaven and hell) in a manner which is only understood in its own environment. And the picture of reality is shifted from tongue to tongue.

They are, conceptually, an equivalent version of the new consciousness in the world today. I claim simply that altered states of consciousness allow people to substitute one symbolic system for another type of thinking about vision, and reality, and about others.

Philosophy – Analysis

At this point our excursion into philosophy and language analysis should be obvious. The Western world system takes on the mark of a symbolic system; one leading to objective truth, theism and naturalism. This system tells us that there is only one way to think. So, the analysis of the cosmic consciousness, and the system of the world, oppose one another.

Physics and Theories for Thought

Many of the proponents of these relativist roots, and their counterparts in our current theories pertaining to the physics of the paranormal, point to a specific version of conceptual relativism where mediums perform the medium mystic tasks and abide by the following basic mystical viewpoints:

a) Mysticism is a better way of gaining information than the senses.
b) There is a fundamental unified understanding of all things.

c) Time is an illusion.
d) At other times, when mediums are ordinary inhabitants of the visible universe, they will accept more commonsense notions of reality.

We can quote deliberately from modern scientists, especially physicians, who call on the notion of common electricity to explain why an electron appears to behave sometimes like array of particles, and at other times like a wave, depending on the instrument they are using to observe it. We know only that it appears in some of our equations as one thing, and in other formulations as another.

Loss of Meaning

From epistemologies, metaphysics, and nihilism we gather together strands to make a rope long enough, and strong enough on which to hang the whole culture.

The real meaning of loneliness is a soul without the knowledge of God's will for direction.

Cosmic Loneliness

"Must everything have purpose?" asked God.
"Certainly," said man.
"Then I leave it to you to think of one for all this," God said, as He walked away.

This may sound funny to the believers, but it shows our human dilemma. We are now in an impersonal universe. The moment a self-conscious, self-determined being appeared on the scene, God gave him choices and left man to make decisions on his own. And man said what is the meaning of all this? What is the purpose of the cosmos? If the cosmos is to have meaning, we must manufacture it for ourselves.

Relativism:

Any theory of ethics, or knowledge based on the idea that all values or judgments are relative and differ according to circumstances, persons and cultures.

Free Will

We have taken ourselves way too seriously. Everyone is consistent with their own set of values. Others affirm a similar set. They appear to know, and do not ask how they know. They just know.

They seem to be able to choose and do not ask themselves whether this apparent freedom is capricious, or deterministic. Socrates said, "The unexamined life is not worth living." But for a naturalist, he is wrong. For, a naturalist it is the examined life that is not worth living.

Heaven, as defined by Webster's dictionary, is a state, or place of complete happiness, or perfect rest attained by the good, after death. Popularly, the abode of God houses angels and the blessed. Any venue of great beauty or pleasure moves heaven and earth to mimic the sublime.

Beyond the Body

The kingdom of heaven is the dwelling place of the Son of God, who left not His Father, and dwells not apart from him. Heaven is not a place, or condition. It is an awareness of perfect oneness, and of the knowledge that there is nothing else. Nothing lies outside of this oneness. And nothing else is within God's time, space, and perfect forgiveness for all things.

Awareness of Heaven

Man's belief that he could have something outside of himself has cost him the awareness of heaven and of his true identity. We have all done this strange thing and not even realized it. We have displaced our guilt, from our minds, to our bodies. Yet anybody cannot be guilty, for he can do nothing of himself. You, that think you hate your body, deceive yourselves. In truth, you hate your mind, for guilt has entered into it.

CHAPTER 15: SALVATION

Salvation

Let us have the instruments of separation be reinterpreted as an indication that we have misunderstood the total salvation approach. We should welcome and improve the shift from fantasies of vengeance, to release from the bondage of those fantasies.

Our perception of our bodies can clearly be sick. But let us not project this sickness upon the total self. Our attempt to destroy what cannot be destroyed can have no real effect at all. Worry is not the answer for any of our problems. God created only what *His* will can destroy. It is insane to use the body as a scapegoat for the guilt that we have attracted. We cannot blame our bodies for that which *we* wished to do. It is impossible to carry out fantasies of self-destruction, for our real selves are indestructible.

Limited Body

The body is a limit imposed upon the universal communication that is an eternal property of the mind. But if we listen closely, we discover that the communication can be internal. The mind reaches to itself, within itself. It has no limits and there is nothing outside of it. It encompasses everything. The body is outside of the real you. It surrounds you. It shuts you off from others. It keeps you from the pure understanding of nature.

Love must be forever pure – changeless forever and ever, without the finite putting a barrier around it. God placed nothing between Himself and you.

Touching Heaven

You can stretch out your hand and touch heaven. You, whose hand is joined with your brother's hand can begin to reach beyond the body. But you need not reach outside yourself to touch your true identity. For the mind is centered within the body. You are surrounded only by God. What limits can there be when He encompasses all.

Everyone has experienced a sense of being transported beyond this earth, and one's self. That feeling of liberation far exceeds the dream of freedom. It is a moment of actual escape from our limitation. One must consider what this transport really entails. A blueprint of yourself – a sudden awareness of the body and the adjoining of yourself to something else which enlarges your mind to encompass it.

Limited Awareness

In this awareness process, what really happens is that you have given up the illusion of a limited awareness and you have lost your fear of the unknown. You have escaped from fear.

FIGURE 26

Escaping Reality

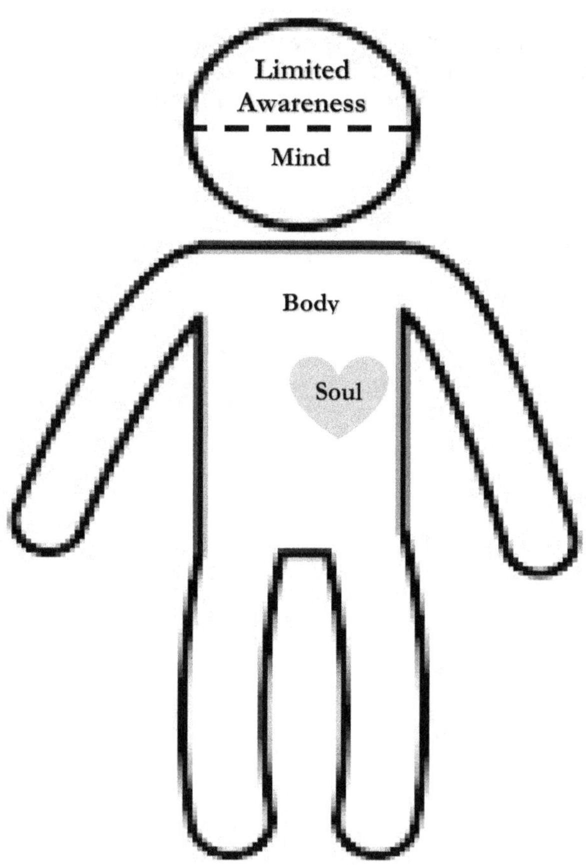

You have escaped from fear, to a place of asking no questions of reality, but merely accepting it. You have finally accepted reality, beyond the body, and have let yourself be one with something beyond limitations.

Sudden Expansion of Awareness

In a holy instant the barriers of time and space have slipped away. You are experiencing peace, joy and the leaving of the body. You are no longer questioning whether it is possible. It is possible because you really want it. The sudden expansion of awareness takes place with your desire for it. It appears irresistibly, in a holy instant, and causes you to be yourself, within its embrace.

Heaven and Resurrection

The resurrection is the overcoming of death on earth. We need to have a real awakening, a rebirth, a change of mind and heart about the meaning of life. And the meaning of death. Heaven is the Holy Spirit's interpretation of the world's purpose. The acceptance of God's plan for atonement is up to us.

FIGURE 27

Learning Salvation

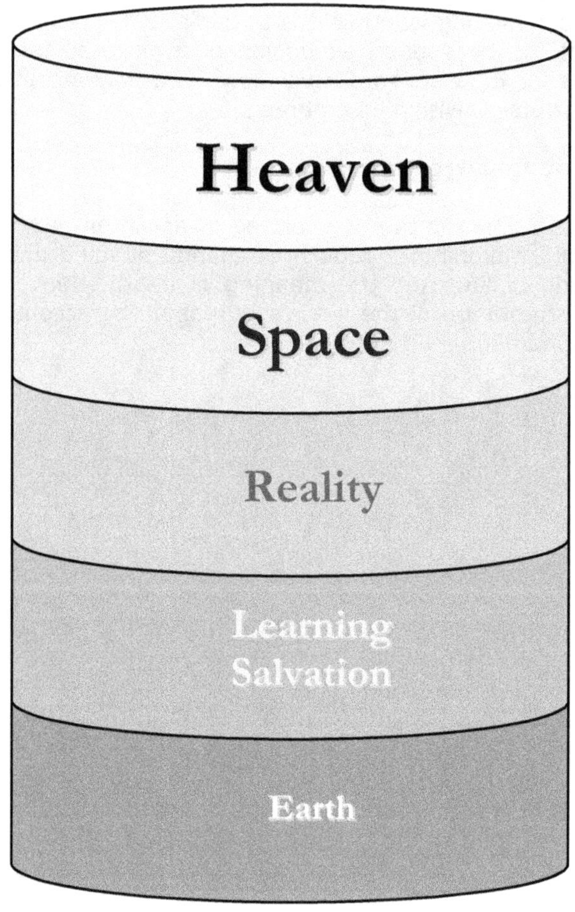

Golden Union

We recognize the true and logical conclusion for who we are. Your union with the spirit beyond, belongs to you. This will extend your joy and happiness on earth, for as long as you maintain that earthly spiritual connection with our higher power. God's will, God's contact, and the Golden Union of spirit manifests mighty works.

You have now realized that it was impossible to understand what felt entirely out of reach before you received this message. Now you have listened to what can never be communicated, when you deny who you are, in faith and in form. You are *something else*, altogether. Your mind has been opened by that *something else*. If you already had vision, this course would not have been necessary. God has no secrets. He does not lead you through a world of misery, waiting to tell you at the journeys end why He worked with you in the way that He did.

Real

We have learned that on earth we do have choices. But sometimes our choices are mismanaged, and we have made mistakes. By now you should understand who you are, and the message that you have received. Understanding this course has opened your mind to infinite possibility.

In each holy approach to this new relationship lies the ability to communicate, rather than separate, from the real. We can now focus on our spirit.

FIGURE 28

Insight to the Spirit on Earth

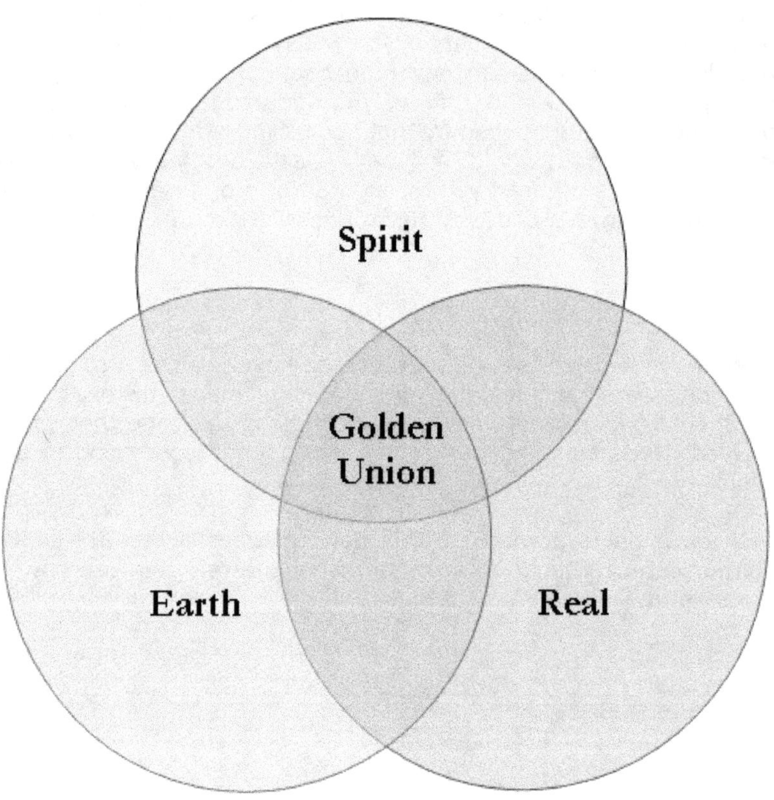

End of Misery

We have ended our dreams of misery and received glad awareness of the Holy Spirit's dream. It is at lesson's end that we found communication and suppressed all of our old judgments.

The resurrection is the denial of death. It is the total assertion of life, where all the thinking of the world is reversed, entirely. Life is now recognized as salvation and redemption. Misery of any kind is perceived as guilt. Love is no longer feared, but gladly welcome.

Our, outdated beliefs have disappeared. And the remembrance of God's contact shines, unimpeded, around the world. Fear and the pain of guilt no longer hold us in darkness. We now stand in the light of forgiveness.

The "Method of Forgiveness" clearly points out the guilt that we all carried. And we needed God's help to remove it. There is no sorrow still upon the earth. The joy of the redeemed man has clearly come upon us.

Heaven and Waiting

These things await us all, but we are not prepared as yet to welcome them with maximum joy. As long as the mind remains possessed of evil, the dream and thought of hell remains real. God's teachings have the goal of waking the minds of those that are asleep. And the vision of Christ takes the place of the dream of hell.

We are redeemed because we have let go of the old judgment of others and self. We are quiet and still. We are able to hear and listen, to God's voice. We are now free because we hear God's voice proclaim the clear truth.

Perception of Awareness

Here is the first direct perception you can make towards awareness of your moment of rebirth. Some of us, in an instance, awaken to what was always there for us. Think what that instant brought. The recognition that what you felt was an illusion was removed in an instant, and you were shown the truth. I hope this shows you that the self is denial and illusion. We call on the truth to deny the illusion of self and to recognize that fear is meaningless.

Interpretation of Meaning

Would God had left the meaning of the world to your interpretations? If He had, it would have no meaning. It cannot be that meaning can change constantly and still be the truth. The golden union of spirit looks upon the world with one purpose, changelessly established. Could change in your current situation be open to a different interpretation, every time you think of it? If so, you would add an element to the script of heaven *that you write* every minute of the day and night. Would your scripts be expected to reflect, based on your own plans, what the day should hold? You judge disaster and success, advance, gain, and loss. Those judgments are made according to the role your script has given you.

All in all, we make judgments with labels that change with our judgment. Escape from earthly judgments. What we fear, and that which we think we want, is not real. Do not maintain the idea that our purpose is the end of all ideals, but to sacrifice our ideals in exchange for those of heaven, without feeling that we have sacrificed anything of value.

End Judgment on Sacrifice

There can be no thought of sacrifice apart from the *idea* of sacrifice. And it is the idea of having different goals that shifts perception and changes meaning. Set one major goal. And that is to allow yourself to agree with God's plans. Then the need for interpretation is lost.

Common Goal

Our common language lets us speak to all our brothers and to understand with them that forgiveness has been given to us all. And this we can communicate again and again.

CHAPTER 16: ATONEMENT FOR FORGIVENESS

Atonement – Forgiveness

Atonement is for everyone, because it is the way to undo the belief that everything is for you alone. To forgive, is to see the other side of where you are, and just a small glimmer of heaven. Look beyond the errors of others and gain a new perception of yourself. In doing so we take away the guilt that makes us sick. We shed the sickness, leaving no vessel for it to come back to.

Dreaming and Healing

You were not healed. You became aware that you were in a dream in which you were sick. You found a magic formula and you were made whole. And yet you have not awakened from the dream. Your mind is exactly as it was before. The difference is the content of the dream. As long as you are on earth, you are stuck in the dream. But now you dream of the reality of your spiritual access to the great beyond.

Getting to heaven is not just the trip and the arrival. It is learning the truth that atonement heals, with certainty, and cures all sickness for the mind that understands that sickness is nothing more than a dream. Sickness is but another form of guilt. Atonement does not heal the sick – for sickness is nonexistent. But atonement heals all guilt.

FIGURE 29

Channelling Healing

We perceive the value of forgiveness to lie solely within the world of religion, which is sought no longer for its gifts, but for forgiveness. True forgiveness is found solely within ourselves. Because no one truly understands this, no one preaches that forgiveness is to be found within ourselves or within our subconscious.

There is instead, a totally misunderstood phenomena going on. We think that we are helping others, or we judge ourselves to be doing the right thing in everything we do. When, in essence, we are seeking God's approval.

Meanwhile, forgiveness eludes us because our inner guilt creates fear. Fear holds us back from all great discoveries. Fear holds us back from all great happenings. It is a mighty demand made upon us by our egos, from which we wish to be set free. But our ego laughs back at us and says, "Hold on to this fear until I say you can let go of it."

In most cases, the ego sets the rules for all our behavior, our thoughts, our emotions, our guilt and our fears. These rules controlled our world and dictated how we were to love others. We really need to understand that the ego was in charge, and that the ego always set the ground rules.

The irony in this is that we ourselves are constantly programming the ego, though we are unaware that we are doing so. Any personal contact with others, and we unknowingly program what the result will be.

We tried hard to change, and we wanted not to feel. And while we tried to analyze our frustration, we still went with the program the ego told us to go with. And we still acted as the programmed ego told us to act. This cycle continued until we completely reprogrammed our ego.

In these lessons we have explained just how, and why, the ego must be reprogrammed. The method for doing so has been presented in this book. This introduction has been but a peek into the dark secret that the ego holds – it thinks that it is in control. We have seen that we can take back that control. We have fully reviewed and analyzed this concept and improved our thoughts on the matter.

In my first book, "The Method of Forgiveness", we simply wanted to say that the first step towards freedom involves a sorting out of our faults and constructing a sensible reflective review of them. This step is not trivial for most people. Everyone will ultimately look upon creation and choose to preserve only what is good in it, just as God did when he looked upon us. What He created was good because He knew what He was doing.

Arriving ultimately at the answers presented in this book, our minds will begin to look with love on this creation because of its worthiness. Without these lessons our minds will ultimately disallow most great things and great thoughts and will hold instead to guilt and pain.

Once more, in approaching forgiveness and surrender by considering our judgments, we must take a hard look at the most frightening part of our decision-making – our youth. By taking an inventory of the choices we made, we will uncover the fact that our decision-making was based on our emotions and find that our thinking was so very negative during that time.

Children are unaware of themselves, because children are only responsible for just being here and doing the best they can. *They* are not – *we* were not... responsible for our total being.

The New Beginning

GLOSSARY

A

Abundance: A fullness of spirit that overflows.

Actions: The process of doing something to achieve a purpose.

Advocate: Someone who acts or intercedes on behalf of another.

Alpha: Alpha rhythm. A pattern of smooth, regular electrical isolations in the human brain that occur when a person is awake and relaxed.

Altruistic: Selflessness; an attitude or way of being, marked by unselfish concern for the welfare of others.

Ambiguity: Uncertainty.

Analysis: The examination of something in detail, in order to understand it better or draw conclusions from it.

At-Oneness: The quality of being one as opposed to many.

Attention Span: The length of time that somebody can concentrate effectively on a task or activity.

Attitude: An opinion or general feeling about something.

Atonement: The making of reparation for a sin or mistake; reconciliation between God and man.

B

Befitting: To be suitable or appropriate for somebody, or something.

Beta: The beta wave is a brain pattern of

brain waves generally found in those awake. Beta waves travel more quickly than Alpha waves.

C

Carotid Artery Surgery
A procedure by which a surgeon gently removes the atherosclerotic plaque that has accumulated inside the internal carotid artery; a large blood vessel which delivers the largest portion of the brain's blood supply. The plaque can generate stroke symptoms by diminishing blood flow to large areas of the brain or by dislodging small fragments which travel into the brain and interrupt local blood flow.

Choices:
A decision to choose one thing, person, or course of action in preference to others.

Condition:
A way of being; a general state or mode of the existence. Especially one characterized by hardship or suffering.

Connection:
The joining together of two or more people, things, or parts. A physical or logical link.

Consciousness:
Awareness of surrounding; somebody's mind and thoughts.

Consequences:
The effect, result, or outcome of something occurring earlier.

Creative Forces:

A phenomenon where a power, energy, or intensity causes something new to be generated, or produced by originality of thought, or convention.

D

Delta: State of sleep from which it is difficult to awaken.

Dissect: Examine in detail; to analyze a person, or subject in detail.

E

Emotionally: Involving an effective state of consciousness, distinguished from cognitive and volitional states of consciousness. Actuated, affected, or determined by emotion rather than reason.

Environment: Surrounding influences.

Expiation: To make amends, show remorse, or suffer punishment for wrongdoing.

F

Faith: Belief in, devotion to your trust in somebody or something; especially without proof.

Feeling: A consciousness, or awareness; motion, or emotional perception, or attitude. An emotional state, or reaction. Easily moved by emotion.

Fundamental: Relating to, or affecting the underlying principles, or structure of something.

G

Guilt: An awareness of having done wrong, or committing a crime, accompanied by feelings of shame and regret.

H

Hearing: To gain information by way of sound. To receive auditory communication.

Higher Power: A power greater than oneself.

Examples include nature, consciousness, existential freedom, science, gravity, Buddha, and God.

I

Imagine: To form a mental image of; to think or believe.

Inferiority: Lower in rank, standing, or degree.

Intellectual: Relating to, or, involving the mental processes of the abstract thinking and reasoning.

Intercession: The action of pleading on somebody's behalf.

Introspection: Observation or examination of one's own mental and emotional state, or mental processes. The act of looking within oneself. The examination of one's own thoughts, impressions and feelings; especially for a long period of time.

Intubation: To insert air to the vocal cords and into the windpipe in order to provide a patient's lungs with oxygen; usually done during surgery, under anesthesia.

J

Judgment: A divine sentence or decision. The process of forming an opinion or evaluation by discerning and comparing. To discern.

K

Karma: The concept of an action, or the calling an entire cycle of cause and effect. Karma is not punishment, or retribution, but simply an extended expression, or consequence of natural acts.

Karmic Influence: Karma is simply something that exists within us, which moves us all and is made up of events that have happened or will happen to us.

L

Liberation:

To release a person, group, population, or country from a population, or country, or military, or political control. To release from severe physical constraint.

M

Materially:

Somebody regarded in terms of his, or her suitability to perform a particular job or task.

Meditation:

Continued or extended thought; reflection; contemplation.

Moral:

Relating to issues of right and wrong, and how individual people should behave.

Mystic:

Involving, or characterized by esoteric, otherworldly, or symbolic practices, or content. Mystic implies obscure or mysterious character, or significance.

N

Negative:

Indicating "no," or refusing or denying something.

O

Occult:

Of, or characteristic of magical, mystical, or supernatural arts, phenomena, or influences. Beyond the range of ordinary knowledge or understanding; mysterious.

P

Pain:

A distressing sensation causing

	physical, mental or emotional suffering, or torment.
Perception:	An attitude or understanding based on what is observed or thought.
Phenomena:	A fact, occurrence, or circumstance observed, or observable that is impressive, or extraordinary. An appearance, or immediate object of awareness in experience.
Physical:	Relating to the body, rather than the mind, the soul or the feelings.
Positive:	Certain, and not in doubt.
Precedent:	An action or decision that can be used subsequently as an example for a similar decision, or to justify a similar action.
Psychic Experience:	A moment of intuition, an expression, or even a gut feeling. When you have a psychic experience, you are receiving information on a nonverbal level.
Psychoanalysis:	A systematic structure of theories concerning the relation of conscious and unconscious psychological processes. A method of studying the mind, and treating mental, and emotional disorders based on revealing, and investigating the role of the unconscious mind.

Q

R

Reality:	Actual being or existence, as opposed to an imaginary, idealized, or false nature. All that exists or happens.
Resentment:	The feeling of displeasure or indignation at some act, remark,

Resolve:

person, etc. Regarded as causing an injury or insult. Resentment can be irritation, envy, or jealousy.

Come to a final decision about something. To find a solution to a problem.

S

Self-aggrandizement: Somebody's personality, or an abstract of somebody's personality, especially as perceived by others.

Self-indulgence: Lack of self-control in pursuing your own pleasure or satisfaction.

Soul: The spiritual part of humans regarded in its moral aspect; the emotional part of human nature; the seat of the feelings or sentiments.

Spiritual: Distinguished from the physical nature and being characterized by a predominance of the spirit; of, or pertaining to sacred things, or matters; devotional; sacred.

Stress Points: Mental, emotional or physical strain caused by anxiety or overwork. It may cause such symptoms as raised blood pressure or depression.

Subconscious: Existing, or operating below, or beyond consciousness. The totality of mental processes of which the individual is not aware; on reportable mental activities.

Surrender: To yield to the possession, or power of another; to give oneself up, abandon, relinquish, submit, or resign.

T

Tenets: Something accepted as important

     truth; an established fundamental belief, especially one relating to religion.

Theists: Belief that one God created, and rules humans and the world; not necessarily accompanied by belief in divine revelation such as through the Bible.

Theta: The eighth letter of the Greek alphabet. Subconscious brain waves.

Thought: That which one thinks; a consideration, or reflection; meditation, contemplation, or recollection; intention, imagination, design, or purpose.

Three-dimensional – mind/body/soul: The body, mind and soul remain intact and connected as long as we are alive. What we must remember is that each of these three parts of us is critically important to the other two parts. We must take care of each of these three parts, individually, to make sure our lives are whole and healthy. When the body does not work properly or is in pain, the mind and soul can be adversely affected. Our body can be made to run at peak efficiency through exercise, optimal health care, nutrition and attention to what our body is telling us. If our body gets sick, we get worn out or run down. We must keep our mind in proper working order by praying, meditating and using mental exercises to keep us alert and thinking young. Our soul must also be kept in proper working order by a deep and abiding faith in God.

Touch: To cause to be briefly in contact, or conjunction with something; to hurt the feelings.

Tranquil: Free firm commotion, or disorder; peaceful, quiet, or calm.

U

Undeniable: Unquestionably true, or real, and beyond dispute.

V

Visualization: A technique involving focusing on positive mental images in order to achieve a particular goal. To recall, or form, from mental images, or pictures. To make perceptible to the mind, or imagination.

Visualize: To recall or form mental images or pictures; to form a mental image of something.

W

Will: A part of the mind that makes decisions; The part of the mind with which somebody consciously decides things

Willingness: Consenting; inclined; cheerfully consenting, or ready.

X

Y

Z

129